After revisiting o...
one night as I sat journali...
room, I dec... to ... an ...
music I was r... d...
And ...e most ...
happened. As ...
came ...my p...
th... ... a...

These a...
...that it's h...
...
life ...
... I re...
new? I don... ...t it to b...
...et me t...ke you ...ly Ca...
...ight? I ... we fi...our...
...t ... ...g... from th...
a ... inde... ...he ...
It ... ...o shift, p...
forward, as long as ...
your heart and you...
...rules that others ha...

Messenger, Lisa
Risk & Resilience
ISBN 9781925283655
First published in 2018 by The Messenger Group Pty Ltd
Editing: Amy Molloy
Proofreaders: Che-Marie Trigg and Rebecca Hooton
Art Direction and Design: Emily Ponton
Photography of Lisa: Scott Ehler
Styling of Lisa: Lydia-Jane Saunders, outfit by Aelkemi
Distribution enquiries: Lisa Messenger, lisam@collectivehub.com

This is proudly a Messenger Group product
lisamessenger.com

DISCLAIMER
The content of this book is to serve as a general overview of matters of interest and is not intended to be comprehensive, nor does it constitute financial (or other) advice in any way. This book is a compilation of one person's ideas, concepts, ideologies, philosophies and opinions. You should carry out your own research and/or seek your own professional advice before acting or relying on any of the information displayed in this book. The author, Messenger Group Pty Ltd and its related entities will not be liable for any loss or damage (financial or otherwise) that may arise out of your improper use of, or reliance on, the content of this book. You accept sole responsibility for the outcomes if you choose to adopt and/or use the ideas, concepts, ideologies, philosophies and opinions within the content of this book.

RISK &
RESILIENCE

BREAKING
AND REMAKING
A BRAND

INTRODUCTION

I always say that when you're deep in the middle of a total and utter, mind-scrambling cluster-f*ck is when the best ideas materialise. I started writing this book in December, 2016, when we were three months off our four-year anniversary for *Collective Hub*. To the outside world, our brand was shining brightly. The magazine's circulation was higher than ever, we were sold in 37 countries, our digital platform was growing rapidly and our events, books and educational resources were consistent sell-outs.

But this is the story of how we very nearly lost everything – truly. This is the reality of how scaling too quickly, hiring too rapidly, over-promising without adequate resources, not employing right-hand people early enough and letting our egos take over, very nearly sunk me.

From the start of *Collective Hub*, I made a promise to be an entrepreneur for entrepreneurs. Anyone who has read my books knows that I don't hold back anything. I wear my heart on my sleeve, my failures for the world to see, and have always vowed to document the ups and downs of being a disruptor.

Well, welcome to my most revealing book yet. A book that's so raw and honest in places that I'm sure most traditional business consultants would call me crazy for lifting the veil and being so honest about what it really takes to make a business work.

The truth is that, as a rebellious and innovative founder carving a new path in an industry verging on crumbling, there are going to be periods when things don't go your way. At best, it might be a blip that lasts a few weeks. In our case, our tough 'patch' lasted for 18 long months and finished with an unexpected twist that shook the media world.

In the end, as you'll read about in (uncensored) detail in this book, my entrepreneurial journey took a bold and unexpected pivot that came about as the result of an insane amount of courage, universal trust, guidance from priceless advisers and inspiration from our incredible community.

Over the next 10 chapters you'll come on a rollercoaster with me. However, this isn't a story of failure or disappointment. The reality? This is what it takes to survive in the start-up scene. At the toughest point for *Collective Hub*, when I revealed my worries to my most trusted entrepreneurial friends, they all responded with the same message: "Oh, we've been there."

These are incredible businessmen and women, many of whom are hailed as saviours of their industries, yet at some point or another they nearly lost it all. Many of them spoke about the same mistakes that nearly led to their destruction.

They grew too quickly, they didn't have adequate systems to support them, their profile didn't match their profit, they hired the wrong people. They didn't seek help – this is a BIG one – and instead buried their heads in the sand, through a mixture of pride, guilt and stubbornness. They didn't admit they had a problem until it was almost too late to overcome it.

These are the times we rarely talk about as founders. Oh, we talk about the bad days, the long nights, and the investor rejections. But we rarely talk about the times when a bad day turns into a bad week, a bad month and even a bad year. During these longer stretches, exhaustion and daily struggles overshadow all the amazing victories that are still happening in your business but start to go unnoticed and, even worse, uncelebrated.

I remember sitting in my office exactly 3.7 years to the day that I started *Collective Hub*. My chest was tight with worry because we were so close to going under but, to the outside world, we were still having so many successes. Earlier that week, my dad had phoned me sounding chipper, asking if I was swinging back in my chair with my feet up on the desk, surveying my "kingdom". I wish that was the case!

Despite new figures showing that our circulation was booming, suddenly everything was heading into an out-of-control shit-storm. I'd just employed a Chief Operating Officer, far too late, in hindsight. Within a week of the COO starting, we had eight resignations. This included a number of my most trusted, long-term team members who had been with me from the beginning, when *Collective Hub* was nothing more than a vision; a scrappy mock-up.

What had changed since those early days? In my experience, in the first three years of any business, approximately, it's risky and scary but you're driven by so much adrenaline you just keep going. The challenges don't engulf you because you have this infectious optimism. The sleepless nights, lack of cash and shoestring resources are still a novelty factor. It's funny and quaint that you can't afford teabags. Every minor win (a $10,000 ad deal or hitting 5000 Instagram followers) is a reason to crack open a bottle of (the cheapest) sparkling wine for your team to celebrate.

If you're a true disruptor, you probably also don't have a lot of competition. When I launched *Collective Hub,* there was no magazine doing anything for entrepreneurs, particularly women. There was certainly no one presenting business content with design flair, like we were. If you're an innovator who's leading the charge, every day is new. You're inventing and changing a landscape, and that's just about the most exciting thing you could ever do…

Then, cracks gradually (or suddenly) start to appear. And, if you don't address them instantly, those cracks become chasms, which can bring down the walls of the castle you've built in the sky and turn your amazing, visionary idea to dust. I know because it very nearly happened to us.

Throughout the hardest 18 months of my business life I kept an uncensored journal. I'll share extracts from it through the next 10 chapters. While writing this book, when I read back through my diary entries, I sound like I'm crazy in places. One moment, I'm flying high and the next I'm sobbing in my car, unable to understand how a business that, in some ways, is bigger and bolder than ever, could also be so fragile, unpredictable and energy-sapping. However, I'm also extremely fortunate and, as I write this, I'm full of gratitude. Despite 18 months of hardship (#understatement), I can now see a silver lining and am incredibly excited about the future, as should you be, too.

I'm so lucky to have experienced adversity in business because, otherwise, how could I keep sharing these lessons with our community? I truly feel like the universe throws me these challenges so I can share the truth, and pass on the knowledge of how to survive, thrive and keep believing in yourself. This book is my gift to you, to celebrate a new start for all of us.

Acknowledging tough times doesn't make you a failure. Even entrepreneurs (as amazing as we are!) are still imperfect, flawed humans on a constant, unending learning curve. When you truly step into your purpose – and I believe I'm on purpose now more than ever – it's so important to have systems and processes (and the right team to complement your weaknesses) to enable you to handle this big beast. Otherwise, it could turn on you.

I hope you can learn from my most painful lessons and, in doing so, future-proof your business from common threats and weaknesses. I also hope that, if and when you do face gruelling challenges, you feel less alone and realise you're not the first person to run into that speed bump. Even in the bleakest, darkest corners of the start-up maze, there's always a way out – if you're willing to retrace your steps, take a new path or ask for help from an experienced guide.

Or, if you're willing to press pause on a project – or even your hero product – and trust that the ensuing time and space will propel you into something much bigger and better. Much more sustainable, with much more longevity.

I won't give the ending away just yet, although perhaps you're already aware of what happened. When a business – especially one born into the spotlight – unveils a dramatic new strategy, it usually makes headlines. Everybody wants to know the reasons behind a new direction, which can seem sudden but is usually the result of months of complex strategies, meetings and negotiations.

For me, I got to the point where I knew only one truth – *Collective Hub*'s purpose must live on in some form. Our research showed that 97 per cent of our readers had taken action to improve their lives after reading something in our print or online articles. That's an incredible legacy that needs to be protected and nurtured.

Am I happy where I am now? Incredibly! I'm grateful for the lessons I learnt, the changes I was forced to make, the end result for my team and the legacy left for our community. I'm thankful that, on a daily basis, I still get emails and messages from *Collective Hub* readers thanking me for enabling them to change their lives and finally ignite their full potential. Isn't that all that matters?

It's you, our wonderful community, who continue to inspire me and guide everything that I do. It's not easy to share your most vulnerable moments, but I trust that you'll go gently with my most intimate memories. I hope that, amid the next 10 chapters, you find hope, courage, resilience and strength. Consider this book a loving supporter and friend, who you can visit whenever you feel troubled or tested.

More than anything, remember you always have choices. As entrepreneurs, it's in our power to choose the risks we take, the people we let into our lives, and the boundaries we set in our businesses. You can choose when to accept a situation and when to exit it, gracefully. You might even surprise yourself with the decisions you make, and that's okay, too.

I'm proud to be one of the many start-up survivors who has been pushed to their limits, and bounced forward again. You have the strength in you to overcome any obstacle. Anything really is possible, believe me.

Much love,

Lisa

Take risks,
dare to
dream,
you are enough
already

To Damian and Jasmin, for helping me to navigate
this journey with smarts, love and loyalty.

CONTENTS

Chapter One

It couldn't
happen to me...
or could it?

CHAPTER ONE
It couldn't happen to me... or could it?

During one of the hardest work weeks of my career, when eight of my trusted team members resigned in seven days and my chief financial officer said we'd be lucky to see the new year (it was November!), I recalled that it was just one month earlier that I'd had dinner with Sophia Amoruso, the original #GirlBoss, the night after she announced her company, Nasty Gal, was not only closing, but filing for bankruptcy.

This auspicious dinner together at North Bondi Fish cemented a friendship that started on social media and had now become a real-world connection. During our catch-up, she was incredibly open, raw, honest and vulnerable with me about what had happened, and the way the news spread across the start-up world. I couldn't have loved her more for how she stood in and owned her truth.

At the time, I'd finally started to accept that I couldn't do all of this on my own, so I'd appointed a new COO and CFO to help me lead the charge at *Collective Hub*. I thought that, with the extra help, my life would soon get easier. After four years of leading the charge myself, I was excited to see where the next stage of my business could take me.

When I heard the sad announcement about Nasty Gal, I remember feeling a surge of empathy and also admiration for Sophia, an amazing business role model. I also remember thinking, 'Thank goodness I'm not there! I don't know how I'd cope if I was in that terrible situation. Wasn't it a US$200million business? How does it go from hero to zero?'

It's incredible, looking back, how far my head was buried in the sand. Although I wasn't facing bankruptcy, *Collective Hub* was no more stable than Nasty Gal at the time in many ways. Ever the eternal optimist, I just didn't want to admit it.

Less than a week later, my newly appointed CFO – who is nothing short of spectacular and, I'm sorry to say, walked into a bit of a shit-storm – looked at me anxiously. "We need to talk," she said. She went on to inform me that, by her estimations, *Collective Hub* would fold in three months if we didn't make drastic changes.

This might seem like a downbeat way to begin chapter one of a book that I promised would be uplifting. But I've never pulled any punches when it comes to speaking the truth about business. And, the truth is that no matter how thriving your customer base, how powerful your product or how wow-worthy your marketing strategy, it doesn't make you bulletproof.

Even the most amazing entrepreneurs in the world have been brought to their knees by a downturn in the economy, a trend change in society, a wave of new competitors or an error in their production schedule.

I'm a firm believer that anything is possible. But there's a flip side to life's ability to constantly amaze and surprise us. The reality is that any business – and every businessman or businesswoman – is flawed and fallible.

Evidence of start-up struggles are everywhere. I'm currently hooked on the podcast, *How I Built This with Guy Raz*, which dives into the stories behind some of the world's best-known companies. There's a common element in all the episodes, whether it's with Maureen and Tony Wheeler from *Lonely Planet*, one of the *Vice* guys, the founder of Whole Foods Market, or Sir Richard Branson. They all seemed to build to a point and THEN had a time when they thought they would lose it all.

Why am I pointing this out? Because, the first step to protecting your business and building your resilience is to admit you might have a problem – if not now, then sometime in the future. The best thing you can do for yourself right now – apart from reading this book – is to really examine your business, identify your weak points, and get REALLY intimate with the issues that could potentially harm you.

As an entrepreneur, there's a duality between having to be the eternal optimist – in order to survive and rise – and also needing to be realistic and very detail-orientated. My superpower skill set has always included being forward-thinking, disruptive and inventive, taking risks and growing a movement. I'm kick-arse good at that, and I always have been.

But you need to balance these with some serious people who can keep all the numbers, checks and balances flowing to counter the crazy. The first question was: had I hired the right people? And the second question was: had I hired these people too late to the party? Turns out that one of them I hit 100 per cent in the 'I got it right' stakes. The other one, I probably couldn't have got more wrong… and it went on to become a very costly mistake.

On good days
laugh,
on tough days
learn

Step One... Let's Talk money!

As you will all know, I'm a firm believer in the adage, 'It's not what happens to us – it's how we deal with it.' We all make mistakes. We all have shortcomings. We all have failures. But we have the opportunity to let them sink us, OR we can use them as learning curves and springboards to propel us into a bigger, brighter future. I wouldn't have survived 16.5 years in business, emotionally, if I kicked myself and punished myself for every disappointment, rejection or ignored email. There's a quote I spotted on Instagram that summed it up beautifully: 'You don't need to be perfect to inspire others. Let people be inspired by how you deal with your imperfections.' How awesome is that?

There are people, even now, who will be reading this book thinking, 'But Lisa, what about your reputation?' They're the old-school thinkers who believe that to survive in business you have to be seen as invincible. Well, I have a message for them. What you've read already is only the BEGINNING – the really gritty details are yet to come, I promise.

In business, nobody is infallible. Take Reid Hoffman, co-founder of LinkedIn, whose original attempt to create a new social media platform failed before he made the version we're all familiar with, which he later sold to Microsoft for US$26.2 billion. A similar story applies to Airbnb's founders, who struggled to gain traction as a profitable platform before hitting the jackpot.

Having a product that people love doesn't mean it's going to be profitable. A good example is Spotify. Despite over 60 million subscribers, the music streaming service has still failed to turn a profit. There are constant rumours swirling that the brand is in trouble. But, in the face of lacklustre revenue or, in this case, a huge cost base, the company has celebrated other victories, such as partnership deals with Warner Music and Microsoft, that have secured its future and pulled it back from closure – at least in the short-term.

Similarly, even in Uber's absolute heyday, it wasn't making a profit. Yet it was THE brand that EVERYONE talked about. Everywhere I went, people were saying, 'Be Uber or be Uberised.' The same applies to SoundCloud, another music-streaming platform which started with a freemium model. When we interviewed co-founder Eric Wahlforss for *Collective Hub*, he revealed their number-one goal is to "empower creative culture". Which is awesome, of course! But is it sustainable as a business model?

In the past two years, SoundCloud's finances have been under scrutiny, with reports the founders were considering a fire sale after being unable to raise enough money to continue operating. They denied these claims and, just a few weeks later, announced they had secured a US$70 million credit line from three investors – Ares Capital, Kreos Capital and Davidson Technology – to "enable SoundCloud to strategically grow".

If you're reading this book, and your ego is saying, 'I'd never get myself into that situation,' here's a warning: even the most glowing businesses can be vulnerable.

In a blog post about his 'greatest business failures', Sir Richard Branson writes, "Whether it is launching companies like Virgin Brides and Virgin Cola that fell flat on their face, making the wrong call on investments, or simply forgetting to return a call or send an email, I have made hundreds of mistakes. I'm sure I'll make many more this year, and learn valuable lessons from every error. Anybody who tells you they don't make mistakes has just made one."

A few years ago I read a survey that found more than one in three families in England are a monthly pay packet away from losing their homes. It's a similar story in America, where a 2016 survey found that 62 per cent of people have zero savings for emergencies such as unexpected medical bills or car repairs.

Unfortunately, I think many start-ups also operate this way. They just about scrape by, knowing they can cover their bills if everything goes to plan. But we all know business is unpredictable and doesn't always flow fluidly. Even if your profits are rising strongly, a delay or unexpected downturn can be catastrophic.

When I recently visited Facebook's San Francisco HQ, in Building 10, where Mark Zuckerberg and Sheryl Sandberg work, I found much of the building is purposefully unfinished, with beams exposed. Apparently, this is to remind staff that, 'Our work here is never done.'

At the front of the social media site's headquarters is a repurposed sign that still has the name of Sun Microsystems, which used to occupy the back of the building. "Instead of spending a bunch of money on fabricating new signage, we took the hacker approach and repurposed the sign that already existed," says Ben Barry, the graphic designer who transformed it into a Facebook billboard. During my tour, when I asked an employee about this, I was told that it's a purposeful reminder to never get too complacent because you're always a sliver away from going under.

Look at the facts. Every issue of *Collective Hub* costs hundreds of thousands of dollars to produce. That always surprises people who think of a print magazine as a cheapish entity – 168 pages of content, bound together. But even when we launched *Collective Hub*, with just three staff members in a tiny office space, our overheads were around AU$3.5 million a year when you took into account salaries, production and distribution, plus contributions from freelancers, photographers and cover images. And remember I was (and still am to this day), the sole owner and shareholder, and have never raised a cent in investment. That's a lot of ads to sell to cover our cost base.

Then there's the cost of any additional, unforeseen expenses. Like the time our pipes burst in the office or I was invited to visit the Condé Nast headquarters in America, but had to cover my own airfare (there are some opportunities you really can't say no to!).

RISK & RESILIENCE

It's difficult, because the only way a founder can make it through the tough times is to be resilient, laser-focused and ignore the doubters. But also be sure to stop, look and listen. Otherwise, an issue can creep up on you.

Don't believe it can all go wrong so quickly? In 2012, Nasty Gal was leasing a 45,000-square-metre distribution centre and bringing in US$100 million in revenue, tripling sales in three years. It topped a list of the 500 top e-commerce performers, beating Apple and Amazon with their compound annual growth hitting a huge 92.4 per cent.

But in 2016, the same year Sophia's marriage ended, Nasty Gal filed for bankruptcy. Revenue had been sharply dropping and Sophia, who had a 55 per cent stake in the company, stepped down from her position.

"When you're in the role of CEO, if things happen in your company, people expect you to know everything, just because of your position," she recalls. "They think, 'How could you let that happen?' There's often no opportunity for you to resolve those things, because you don't know [about it]."

Since then, she's gone on to do amazing things – which just shows a downturn can happen to the best visionary. A few months after announcing bankruptcy, more than 500 women came together in Los Angeles for the Girlboss Rally – a day of talks and activations to inspire women to rise up and redefine success for themselves. Far more than just a snappy book title, Girlboss Media is now a media company that enables women to connect across social, digital and experiential platforms to share knowledge about their careers, finance, relationships and businesses. (In fact, *Collective Hub* and the Girlboss platform have been content-sharing and are firm advocates for each other.)

To date, the Girlboss Foundation has awarded more than US$130,000 in financial grants to women in the worlds of design, fashion, music and the arts to help fund their passion projects. Clearly, Sophia has an innovative mind, tenacious spirit and the all-important likability factor. Yet, still she found herself at the bitter end of business.

Every challenge is a chance to practice resilience. Be grateful.

Where is your weak spot?

The biggest danger to many brands is their illusion of invincibility. This, according to Bryce G. Hoffman, the author of the book *Red Teaming: Transform your Business by Thinking like the Enemy*, who was interviewed for a past issue of *Collective Hub*. The author, quite incredibly, embedded himself in a US military training facility to learn the strategies the army uses to pinpoint its weaknesses and forecast possible failings.

"The CIA started its version of Red Teaming, called 'The Red Cell', on September 12, 2001. They were still pulling bodies out of the Twin Towers," explained Bryce. "I've talked to folks in the Pentagon who have said that [before this], the prevailing view was that America's technological superiority was so great that it was enough to ensure we could win any war and protect ourselves at home for the foreseeable future. On September 11, 2001, they found out just how wrong they were. The director of the CIA said we weren't as smart as we thought we were."

As a business consultant, Bryce began to look for a way to help companies develop the discipline of forcing themselves to constantly stress-test what they're doing. That led me to discover Red Teaming. "Companies become victims of their own success very easily," he said. "That's one of the things I discovered, particularly [from] companies that have gone through near-death experiences. They turn the corner and say, 'Great, we've solved that problem. Now we can rest on our laurels.' But that creates a new set of problems."

So, what's the antidote? The first step to exposing hidden threats, according to Bryce, is to recognise that, "You don't know what you don't know." One of the things he learnt in Red Teaming training is that no matter how smart we are, no matter how well educated and successful in business we are, we all fall victim to an array of blind spots and biases that skew our decision-making in ways that we can't prepare for ahead of time.

I learnt this – the hard way. When *Collective Hub* launched, we were a small fledgling start-up with minimal staff and minimal touchpoints. It was hard NOT to be across every fragment of the business, because every conversation, whether it was about partnerships, finance or content development, happened in clear sight – and clear sound – in our small office. It was exciting and in the moment. But as we grew larger and our company more complex, the result was less communication and, subsequently, less awareness. I'm the first person to blame! I should have pressed my team for more analytical updates, project reports, statistics, analytics, data and budgets. Instead, I didn't have all the information to see the real danger coming – until it was right on top of us.

At this time, *Collective Hub* had experienced a period of growth beyond my wildest dreams, in terms of reach and products. We'd expanded into 37 countries, sold in thousands of newsagents across Australia, as well as Coles and Woolworths supermarkets. We'd launched a digital version on Press Reader and you could purchase issues through Zinio. We'd held more than 200 events, in locations ranging from health retreats to global conferences and the Australian HQ of Facebook. Every day, I had dozens of emails from brands desperate to collaborate with us.

The irony is, I've written entire chapters in my previous book about the importance of falling in love with data, and unleashing your inner geek. But in this period of immense growth I let my focus wane. There were so many avenues, side products,and contributors to keep track of. I knew our community was growing – rapidly – and were happier than ever with our product, which was my priority. But I had no idea how we were truly performing, financially – or what could be around the next corner. I was focused always on the growth of the brand, our community and the big picture. I sidestepped some of the detail. And I didn't have the right 2IC in place to complement my weaknesses and keep it together. I can do ANYTHING and sell ANYTHING with enough of a 'runway'. But, when your CFO says, "We won't be able to pay wages next month," and you only have three weeks to find a solution, there's no space to think calmly and soundly.

One of the first things I did after that shocking meeting was to ask an amazing founder I know to send me examples of the financial reports that he gets from his management team, on a weekly and daily basis. Then I asked my staff to emulate them. I don't think they were happy about it (I was meant to be the fun-time boss!). But it was essential for us to be able to move forward.

'By failing to prepare, you are preparing to fail,' as Benjamin Franklin once said. The biggest threat to my business wasn't our fast growth, inexperienced (very young!) team or emerging competitors. It was my own inability to see our vulnerability. And that's what I want to save YOU from.

The good news is, you can acknowledge the possibility of failure, without fearing it. You can learn from other people's mistakes and coping mechanisms, without losing your determination. You can be optimistic and realistic, too.

It's time to put aside any illusions of invincibility. There's no point reading this book from a self-built pedestal, secretly believing that you're magically safe from threat and failure. The truth is it CAN happen to anyone. It could happen to you. It nearly happened to me!

One of the reasons I'm writing this book is to help to future-proof your start-up – and your sense of self – from the reality of what could (but I hope won't) be around the corner. To be an entrepreneur takes tenacity, drive and self-belief, an abundance of hope and an anything-is-possible attitude. But to survive the start-up jungle also takes a sensible amount of caution, precision, realism and attention to detail. This doesn't need to be your strength. If it's not, you need a right-hand person who operates that way – their salary is worth it!

As I learnt, being the ultimate optimist and giving your team and your community everything that they desire can be a recipe for disaster. I'm not a person who regrets anything, so I don't wish I did anything differently (what's the point in that?). But I do want to save you from repeating the same mistakes I did. Have you had enough of a reality check? Okay, we'll begin our lessons…

"By failing to prepare, you are preparing to fail"

– BENJAMIN FRANKLIN

6 LESSONS FROM THE KNIFE-EDGE

NEVER THINK YOU ARE BULLETPROOF
The moment you become complacent or comfortable
is the moment it all starts to collapse around you.

DATA IS CRITICAL
You can fight any fight with enough passion and drive, but you need to
know where to focus your energy and block the holes in your company.

GET THE RIGHT PEOPLE AROUND YOU!
Someone who can help you to execute, someone who will
always question you, someone who can control your madness
and someone you can cry with.

SAY NO MORE OFTEN
Don't feel guilty saying no. Focus on the things that are
going to make you great and say no to everything else.

DON'T BE LED BY YOUR EGO
Especially if you're in the public eye in any way. Don't make decisions
based on what an anonymous troll says about you. Always act with
your community in mind – and consciously build a community that
is empathetic and forgiving.

BE GRATEFUL EVERY DAY
Appreciate what has already happened and what might be ahead
(yes, even on the toughest days).

Chase your joy, find your tribe, hope for more

Purpose is a superpower.
Passion helps you fly

Chapter Two

When reality
sets in...

CHAPTER TWO

When reality sets in...

In retrospect there were a number of signs, messages and milestones that marked my journey to, 'Oh f*ck, we're in real trouble.' Interestingly, most of the real signals that should have rung alarm bells were not numbers on a spreadsheet. They were personal, emotional and psychological shifts, which showed up in my life, inside and outside of the office.

In 2016, I found myself absolutely beyond exhausted. I was sick to death of selling my soul – without taking a salary for more than two years – and being on and off planes every week at the mercy of work commitments. Even the part of my job I loved the most – meeting our incredible community at events across the country – had begun to zap my morale and my energy. I had put everything on hold – a relationship, a baby, and all of my precious self-care rituals. In a year, I lost more than AU$1.3 million of my personal money (more on that later) and, after seven years of living in homes that I owned, I had to move into a rental property after selling my main home in Bondi.

"Oh, but isn't she a millionaire?" This is what one of my team had said that her sister had asked with shock (she must have told her how I was living). I could understand her confusion. I revealed – extremely honestly – in my previous book, *Money & Mindfulness*, how I can often make AU$12,000 in a day from a speaking gig.

I've done the maths. If I was a solopreneur right now, simply publicly speaking and writing books for a living, then I would be bringing in up to AU$2 million a year... just for me! But instead, every cent that I personally earned was being pumped into *Collective Hub* to allow us to expand, evolve and produce the top-quality product that our readers know us for.

I was proud that, after 16.5 years of running my own start-ups, I had NEVER needed to get a business loan, and I was not keen to go down that route. But *Collective Hub*, as it stood, was clearly unsustainable if it continued without changes.

To add insult to injury, when I moved out of my beloved home and into a smaller property, one of my financial advisers questioned my decision to paint the place to brighten it up, because she saw it as "unnecessarily expensive". That evening, I wrote in my journal, "The amount of money I bring into this company day after day after day and I'm about to live in a tiny investment property which I get questioned about painting. It's a hard pill to swallow."

She wasn't wrong to question my interiors decision, but it felt like another blow at a time when I was vulnerable, depleted and desperately looking for a pick-me-up. I was giving up EVERYTHING in the name of building an incredible brand and platform to showcase incredible individuals and brands around the world, and inspire others on their own journey.

Side note... I'm currently sitting in Perth doing the last edit of this book and I want to tell you the following to demonstrate the point. I'm here doing three events in three days. A one-night event at AU$250 a head for 125 people. A lunch at AU$375 a head for 10 people. And a paid speaking gig at a discounted rate of AU$6000 as I'm here already. So this trip has brought in AU$41,000 in three days. In addition, I sold more than AU$3000 of books and *Collective Hub* masterclasses. This trip is ALL 100 per cent attached to me and my personal brand. So that's AU$44,000 in three days.

Yet THIS is the reality of the situation. I flew economy booked on points. I stayed in a hotel that we did a contra deal with. And I was booked back on a flight today, which means my day looks like this: Check out of hotel at 11am. Speaking gig is not until 7pm, so I'm displaced for eight hours. Then flight at 11pm Perth time, which equates to 2am Sydney time. Landing

at 6am Sydney time. This means I have to find somewhere to hang out for eight hours, unsexily find somewhere to get changed to get up in front of a room of 200 people and inspire them, then get straight on a flight in the MIDDLE of the night!!!!

How can I bring in so much money, yet be doing this to myself? How can I inspire people when I'm having to put myself second all the time? I could be doing one of these gigs a month and live like a king. BUT, instead, at the moment all I do is work like this to funnel every single cent into keeping *Collective Hub* afloat – and it's taking its toll financially, physically and emotionally.

That's fine in year one, two or even three of a start-up... but quickly approaching year five? This is what you call 'for the love of business'. Only, as time went on, I wasn't loving it any more. I was starting to get very, very resentful. I was starting to begrudge every cent that I had to sacrifice for the sake of the brand. I was depleted and wondered how much more I had to give.

This is not an uncommon story, as I discovered when I started talking to more and more of my colleagues, other founders and successful entrepreneurs. It seems the trajectory I was on was often par for the course. Also, having had businesses for 16.5 years, I've been through this trajectory once before.

As I shared in my book *Money & Mindfulness*, when I launched my first start-up in 2001, I spent the first three years over-servicing and undercharging. By about year three I got resentful and realised I had to make some real changes, starting with upping my fees and starting to say 'no' to unreasonable clients. It was a feeling rather than a financial forecast that alerted me to the problem – and the same was happening this time around.

What are some early signs to recognise your start-up is in trouble? This question appeared on the website Quora and the answers, posted by entrepreneurs and business advisers, were revealing. One respondent,

Bonnie Foley-Wong, the CEO of Pique Ventures and author of the book *Integrated Investing*, wrote a full list of the signs she's seen in sinking start-ups she's encountered.

1. Your investors provide you with advice, which you ignore, then your investors lose interest and stop offering help.

2. As the CEO, you're spending more time winning awards, mentoring other people and travelling to speak at conferences, while your own start-up doesn't grow.

3. As the CEO, you don't understand the numbers (and have no desire to figure out the numbers).

4. Dependency on [your] first and only customer for a long time and you get very comfortable and complacent.

5. You've built your start-up to offer X, but paying customers don't want X, they want Y, which you could deliver on, but you ignore the pivot opportunity in hopes that customers will want X.

6. You believe in 'build it, they will come'. When they don't come, you build another thing with the same approach of 'build it, they will come'.

7. Other ecosystem, infrastructure, or customer behaviour pieces are missing, so your first-to-market strategy is much too early.

8. When something doesn't go to plan or you get some negative feedback, you get irate, angry at anyone within earshot, and either freak out or panic.

You may or may not agree with everything on this list (it's just one person's opinion, of course). According to the online world, which is full of blog posts on the topic, 'Signs your start-up is in trouble', there are common sign posts leading your way to potential disaster. They include closed doors, poor communication and something called 'management opacity'. According to Dele Lowman Smith, founder of American advisers, Bold Move Consulting, this is when "issues are present and managers and leaders fail to address it promptly and candidly".

Other signs include a dip in staff morale (I noticed, at *Collective Hub* HQ, we had empty desks at 10am which would never have happened previously). Then comes resignations from your executive team who, if you're lucky, will be honest about the reasons they're leaving ("I just need more job security"). You know you're REALLY in trouble when you envy them being able to leave. I remember when one of my key team members – who had been with us since the start – said she was leaving, secretly thinking, "How can I blame her? If I didn't own the company, I would go too." It was my fault. I was just so busy trying to survive by this stage that I didn't always have the energy to nurture my beautiful team.

Let me make one thing clear. These aren't all signs your business is going to go down in flames. But they ARE signs you probably need to make some changes, and shouldn't ignore the clues that you have glitches in your company culture. Don't panic! You're probably not at the point of no return. But the sooner you address key issues, promptly and proactively, the sooner you can return to a workplace of productivity, unity and fulfilment.

When negative feelings arise – especially exhaustion, frustration or panic – it's also important to stop and ask: Am I just having a bad day or is this a regular occurrence? Honestly, when you read my journal I sound like a crazy person. One day I'm up and then I'm down. One day I'm walking on air and the next I'm threatening to run away to a deserted island.

A lot of this has to do with the situation I'm in at the time and my environment. When I'm at a speaking gig – actually connected in person to our beautiful community and getting paid fairly for the output – I'm often walking on air. BUT when I'm back in the office trying to convince a 19-year-old at a media agency why they should advertise and they're trying to beat me down to $3000 for an ad... then no... I feel like SHIT. Even though I count myself as incredibly resilient and emotionally buoyant in every way, I'm only human, too. As soon as I'm in the minutiae and small-minded thinking, I am sinking...

Some of my journal rants, I know, were just written on a bad day, sparked by tiredness, the time of the month, the cycle of the moon, a traffic jam I got stuck in, or some tiny event which, in a moment of vulnerability, flipped me from calmness to 'I can't cope-ness'. I've always been the queen of flipping my mindset – in a good way – from negative to positive. So, it was an alien and uncomfortable feeling when my attitude began to flip in a pessimistic direction.

Compared to most people, I was still a shining beacon of optimism. If you've read my book *Life & Love* you'll know how hard I've worked to build a toolkit of rituals and strategies to keep a (genuine!) smile on my face, even during tough times. I could still tap into gratitude. I've honed my routines and rituals and know my trigger points so that I can pull myself out of most slumps pretty quickly... and this is an imperative in this time.

In brainstorming sessions with my staff, I still bounced off the wall with ideas (much to their amusement!), and I still counted myself as extremely lucky to be living a life I'd purposefully created (clearly, all those self-development courses, yoga classes and motivational podcasts were worth it!).

However, there were also repetitive, negative patterns I couldn't ignore, even though I tried to. The kind of thoughts that regularly wake you up in the night, not with a sudden surge of panic but a never-ending sense of dark aboding. How can I afford my staff's salaries this month? Have we overstretched ourselves? Why do I feel so incredibly lonely in my business?

When the same glaring message disrupts the calmness of your mind, over and over again, you simply can't ignore it. According to research, the average human produces up to 50,000 thoughts a day and 70 to 80 per cent of those are negative. That translates to up to 40,000 negative thoughts every 24 hours!

Realistically, we can't take every one of these thoughts seriously (how exhausting!). Instead, we all have to learn how to filter our thoughts and separate the ones we can allow to fly in and fly out from the thoughts that carry a deeper meaning.

How can you do that? There are a whole heap of strategies to practice. The simplest is some form of meditation. You've probably experienced how much calmer your mind is when it's quiet. Sit for a moment and imagine your mind is a big, white cinema screen. Without judgement, allow thoughts to float across the screen – perhaps forming pictures and words. Don't overthink it, just allow them to materialise and then disappear again.

Psychologists also recommend recognising 'thought distortions' – when your mind convinces you that something isn't true, or that something is true which actually isn't. This shows up when we catastrophise and think 'I'm going to lose everything', when in fact there's no evidence that backs up that mental angst.

Sometimes you'll realise that your mind is tricking you into panic. Is your relationship really in trouble or is your spouse just grumpy after a long and difficult work week? Is your product really terrible, or is your ego just wounded from one bad review? Is your employee really leaving because you're a terrible boss, or because she's been offered a pay rise and is saving so she can get onto the property ladder?

Once you've filtered these faux worries, you can focus on the real problems – your weak spots, your brand risks and the issues that could really crush you – and then you can take proactive steps to find a solution. Over the next few chapters, I'll reveal exactly what that solution became for me (and why it was a pivot that I never predicted!).

But first I have to express the importance of the step before the solution. The most important message I want to get across in this chapter is that it's okay to admit the warning signs are there. I only discovered later that a sizeable portion of the anxiety, stress and unease I felt during that time was caused by avoiding our issues; feeling shame, guilt and fear about what people would think if I admitted that we needed to adjust our business model. It takes a HUGE amount of energy to ignore issues and sweep them under the carpet.

One day – December 19, 2016 – after an absolutely sleepless weekend racking my brains, I came in and had a meeting with one of my senior staff members. A plan suddenly materialised in my mind. As I'll explain in the next chapter, it became clear that we needed to move our goalposts and build towards a new future with an updated brand strategy.

And so it began. Right there and then, just when I thought I had nothing more in me, we started the build of my life! I walked out of the office at 4pm the night before Christmas Eve the only way I was going to allow myself to – feeling more proud, more together and more ready for 2017 than I ever could have hoped for.

I had crossed every 't' and dotted every 'I', and I had well and truly set us up for the best chance of success that I could hope for. And like that, I closed my computer and didn't have one bit of stress for eight entire days. I went and hung out with my family. I laughed. I slept. I was present.

Even though we were a long way from being out of the shit, for the first time in a long time I felt like it was going to be okay. It was Mark Twain who said, "Eat a live frog every morning, and nothing worse will happen to you the rest of the day." Well, I had ended my year by eating every frog that I could get my mouth around. And they didn't taste quite as terrible as I thought they would.

It can be hard, as a founder, to admit that something isn't working. Our businesses are our babies and nobody wants to say there's anything wrong with their creation. But addressing your issues is also the most incredible, liberating, empowering and optimistic gift that you can give yourself, your customers and your staff.

In the midst of my toughest week, I emailed one of my most trusted friends, who has achieved incredible things with his personal brand and inspired many people with his teachings. With his permission, I'd love to share the email he sent back to me – an email that I will always treasure close to my heart and re-read whenever I'm doubting my path, dreams or ambitions.

Sometimes you need someone else to remind you what it's okay to feel. I hope that it helps you as much as it helped me. And, to my dear friend and confidant,

Thank you from the bottom of my heart.

" It's wonderful to think we've been friends for 12 years and no change. And it's because we're friends, and because I've been in similar places myself, that I will always have your back.

Rest assured you really are doing all the right things — investing in your dream, thinking through all your options, having difficult conversations, making tough calls and using your current situation as inspiration for a new book are all EXACTLY what a top-tier leader and creative talent would do. Bravo!

It certainly feels lovely to be recognised as someone special. But, as you well know, the reality is that it can be lonely and painful at the top. After all, who can you really talk to when you are hurting or anxious? I know I've struggled with this myself over the years, and I was very lucky to have a friend and flatmate — someone who had been though vaguely similar situations himself when he was younger.

You can bet that no one else wanted to hear that I was stressed, possibly depressed and certainly feeling sorry for himself; no one wanted to hear how a millionaire had money concerns; or that a supposed charismatic force of nature was facing an employee revolt in his own studio... but all these things were very real and likewise very difficult to deal with. Those of us enjoying rare air today know what it takes to get where we are, but few others do, or ever will. I will never be unkind or dismissive towards employees or colleagues, but I have stopped assuming that everyone knows what I know, or that they can understand, see and feel what I understand, see and feel.

Having experienced the highs and lows of running a creative business, I try very hard to be compassionate and communicate clearly — but my family is my family, my friends are my friends, and my employees are my employees. It's dangerous, delusional and even a little pathetic if you confuse these three — trust me on that.

And trust yourself. Always.

When times are tough I choose my confidants carefully, and I am very grateful for their expertise and insight. However, I am not just the captain of my ship — I AM the ship, just as you are your ship, too.

Like storms and summer breezes, valued crew members come and go — but you will remain and the sea will still be calling.

Likewise, in life and business, every safe harbour is guarded by a jagged reef — most people stay inside for their entire existence. To reach beyond the horizon means that you first must sail dangerously close to the coral teeth, risking damage and terrible loss. Less courageous crew will abandon ship, but you must let them swim to shore and carry on.

For once you have tasted the endless opportunities of the open ocean, how can you ever settle for a tiny harbour town?

As you well know, there are many ways to find great happiness, some paths are easy and others less so. However, risk and fear and pain cannot be avoided if you wish to accomplish great things.

Yes, there are always dark perils lurking in the deep, but that is why we navigate by the stars. Look up, stay true and go forward.

I flatter myself when I say that I see the best of myself in you and what you are doing... for you have skills that I don't and you are achieving things that I never could.

You've got this!

Invest in your dream, have difficult conversations, make tough decisions; use every situation as inspiration

8 Signs your start-up is struggling

1. Tiredness is normal. Exhaustion isn't – especially when you wake up every single day feeling like you've been run over by a steamroller.

2. Scan your body – it's the best barometer for stress and anxiety. Are your shoulders tense? Is your stomach tight? What's at the root cause of your discomfort?

3. How is staff morale? If your (usually insanely dedicated and enthusiastic) team are beginning to pull sickies, postpone meetings and complain more it's probably for a reason.

4. You're clinging to a certain outcome, whether it's a project you've decided HAS to happen by a certain date or a prospective employee you HAVE to convince to join you. Why the neediness?

5. Your CFO has a worried look on their face – constantly!

6. On a weekly basis your negative thoughts are beginning to outweigh the positives. You're usually THE most positive person on the planet. What's shifting? And when did it begin to change?

7. You don't want to talk about your work anymore. In fact, you'd rather talk about ANYTHING aside from it.

8. When someone asks why you love what you do, you can't come up with an answer.

Chapter Three

Scale down
(fast)

CHAPTER THREE
Scale down (fast)

In 2016, three of my most trusted department heads kept saying to me, constantly, "We need more staff, we need more people." They weren't the only ones. I was hearing it from six direct reports, all saying the same. "We need more help. Can we please hire someone?" It was my fault, completely, what happened next. Instead of sitting back and taking time to assess our systems and processes, as a people-pleaser, I wanted to make my people happy.

In 11 months, I hired nine more staff, adding a staggering AU$983,000 in salaries to our bottom line in the process. To put that in perspective, our annual base salary in January, 2016 for 16 people was AU$1,245,400. In December, 2016, it had rocketed to AU$2,124,400 for 26, including on-costs for superannuation, payroll tax, worker's comp, etc.

Then, because our office was literally overflowing with people (we were sitting two to a desk!), I decided we needed to move to a bigger office. Instead of a modest upgrade, we went BIG (as is often my mentality). I've done this a few times since the launch of *Collective Hub*, but this time was my most daring move yet.

Call me crazy, but I found myself signing a five-year lease on a 600-square-metre office space in one of the most sought-after areas of Sydney – for AU$236,795 per annum, plus GST, with a 4.25 per cent increase year on year. That meant year two would cost us AU$246,858.79. On top of a bond of AU$59,198.75. Plus two car spaces that cost in rent the equivalent of a studio apartment. This is the PERFECT example of a pivotal moment. If I had hired a CFO earlier, they would have hit me over the head and said no way!!

In my defence, it was an amazing space; a penthouse with a vast balcony space that wrapped around the building. It took up an entire floor of a building in Surry Hills. It was incredibly light, bright and inspiring, with floor-to-ceiling glass windows. As a shell it was breathtaking, but we didn't stop there.

We completely gutted it and rebuilt it from the ground up. We filled it with inspiring wall art, comfortable desks, cosy sofas for brainstorming and put fake turf on the balcony so we could picnic in the sunshine. I have always said it's important to create an inspiring place to work that enlivens your senses, but the entire fit-out cost more than AU$145,000 in total, including furniture, extra walls and kitchen equipment.

Not to mention the high-end interior stylist that I let someone engage in my absence. With the best of intentions, one of my team had signed a complex and rather watertight contract on my behalf, which means we were charged AU$25,000 even though we severed ties. Before we broke that contract, all we got was one table – so, if you think about it, that one table is now worth AU$25,000.

We did some crazy, crazy shit and all because I took my eye off the ball and let things escalate. I knew from the moment I signed the lease on that space that I had made a big, big mistake. Deep down, it just didn't feel right and while it had always been part of the plan to have an actual multi-purpose community 'hub', what's the old adage? Building always costs so much more than you could ever imagine.

Suddenly, my shoestring start-up which – although profitable (just) was only in its third year of business – had to cover a monstrous bill (all approved before my poor new CFO joined the company). I'm all for thinking big, expanding and having the courage to take leaps in business. But in retrospect, my dramatic scaling up was driven by the wrong reasons. And at the time I didn't have the right 'sensibles' around me... I listened to outside chatter saying what I 'should do'; I wanted to make everyone else happy and I forgot the power of 'no' when it comes to conscious business decisions. If I'd taken the time to analyse what my staff really needed, I would have found we didn't need all those people (although adding maybe one or two extra team members would have been sensible.) We certainly didn't need to update EVERY piece of furniture in our office.

In hindsight, at the time we were working inefficiently, which isn't a criticism of my amazing team, but of my flawed leadership. I was used to managing a team of three. When I first launched *Collective Hub*, myself and employees number one, two and three, lived and worked in each other's pockets.

We had constant conversations, brainstorming sessions and nothing happened in the brand without everyone else knowing about it. This meant that we were also super-efficient because our communication channels were so open. Unfortunately, as *Collective Hub* had grown, unavoidably, people weren't talking as much any more.

People were duplicating tasks and doing the same job without realising it; ending emails about the same topics and trying to solve the same problems, separately, without sharing ideas or resources. There were probably three people doing the same job, except I didn't realise it. Instead, everyone felt increasingly strained, overworked and under-supported.

You can understand why I thought more staff – and therefore a bigger workspace – was the answer. I just wanted to love everyone! Whether through ego or pride, I wasn't honest enough with them to say, "We don't have the spare money for this."

It took my business consultant, Damian (my lifesaver, who this book is dedicated to), to point out the obvious. In a (very!) frank meeting, he pointed out that I'd added a fortune to my annual salary outlay and yet our profits had not really grown since I actioned the expansion. We certainly hadn't boosted our revenue in line with the extra people.

This is an extract from my journal I wrote during that period…

> *"I've come to realise in one week of hell, that no one will ever really realise what you are going through unless they have skin in the game. I've been in a constant groundhog day of, 'Can we have more staff?', 'Can we have more budget?', 'Can we have, can we have, can we have?' When you're personally losing $150,000 a month, but you can't quite pinpoint why, you just know your business is incredibly inefficient somewhere (as it turns out, everywhere!) and you have to go from being the fun 'yes' person to the grumpy, broken-record 'no' person. It's absolutely soul-destroying and exhausting."*

Yet I'm not alone in going through this transition. How many entrepreneurs expand and scale for all the wrong reasons? Whether it's because of outside expectations, inside pressure, ego, pride or a warped belief that we need a certain material attribute to seem successful. A big team, a huge office, a company car for each senior staff member, a complete redesign of their packaging for no real reason. I have come to learn that smaller is better. Less is more.

It's very tempting to keep adding, and adding and adding, without consciously assessing your decisions. Your competitor has hired an external PR agency. Do you need one, too? Another start-up in your space has developed an app. Should you have one just because they do? In your existing office, there's nowhere glam to shoot impressive Instagram stories. Is that really enough of a reason to call your estate agent?

Scaling too quickly is the number one reason for 'start-up death', according to a report by Startup Genome on why small businesses fail. After analysing surveys from 3200 start-ups, they concluded that, of the majority of start-ups that failed, 70 per cent fail because of premature scaling, defined as "spending money beyond the essentials of growing the business (hiring sales personnel, expensive marketing, perfecting the product, leasing offices, etc.) before nailing the product/market fit."

It's shockingly easy to grow too fast for your own good, even if you're an experienced business person. Although start-ups, by their nature, are designed to grow fast, to pivot rapidly and have unlimited potential, unsustainable scaling can be the downfall of the strongest business model.

In the last couple of years, there's been a rise in start-ups who have folded after insanely successful crowdfunding campaigns. Their downfall? Their prototype sounded so amazing, and so impressive, that too many customers put in an order. But, they didn't have the processes or raw materials to handle such mass production. I recently listened to a Tim Ferris piece on this – he has stopped promoting start-ups as his numbers are so big when he promotes them they're unable to keep up with the orders… crazy!

In 2017, the chief of Asian tech company, Xiaomi – dubbed the 'Apple of China' – admitted they "grew too fast", after showing a drop in sales in 2016. In an open letter to staff, Chief Executive Lei Jun said, "In the first few years, we pushed ahead too fast. We created a miracle, but also drew on some long-term growth. So we have to slow down, further improve in some areas and ensure sustainable growth for a long-term future."

A certain amount of growing pain is normal, but only until a point. In the TED talk, 'Why Scaling Up Always Hurts', entrepreneur Pete Bell argues that when rapid growth happens in start-ups (which he refers to as 'doubling'), entrepreneurs are often unprepared for the side effects.

"Every time you double, something breaks," he says. Which is fine if you have the strategies, processes and people in place to strengthen the weak point – but we didn't.

As I learnt the hard way, bigger isn't always better, productivity has nothing to do with team size and an inspiring work space doesn't rely on the diameter of your office. I wish I'd listened to the podcast *Masters of Scale with Reid Hoffman* before I scaled up so quickly. In one episode, featuring Airbnb co-founder Brian Chesky, the entrepreneur revealed his belief that, if you want your company to truly scale, you first have to do things that don't scale. Handcraft the core experience. Get your hands dirty. Serve your customers one-by-one. And, stay intimately involved as a founder.

And so, after proudly proclaiming "*Collective Hub* is expanding," I made the incredibly tough decision to scale down – fast! Some of the damage couldn't be undone overnight (like our office issues!) but I could immediately address the inefficiencies and duplications in the business. In short, it was time to think – and act – like a bootstrapped start-up again.

Sometimes it pays to get an outside opinion from someone you trust. During a meeting with Damian, we looked at all the financials of the business. He spent an hour with me and another hour with my Chief Financial Officer (I no longer had a COO by this time), then returned a week later with suggestions for how to slice, dice and reset our model. To embrace his advice, I had to surrender, let go and detach from outcome. In simple terms, he wanted me to FOCUS.

In line with his advice, I divided my scale-down strategies into a number of different areas:

The Magazine How could we tighten our processes and streamline our content creation?

The Events How could we make them more formulaic (in a good way!) and market our most successful events to a wider audience, rather than trying to create new events that were expensive to develop?

The Office

How could we share the space, and therefore the cost, in a positive way that would actually benefit our community? (This lead to us opening the *Collective Hub* co-working space – a dream I'd actually had for years.)

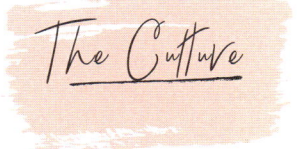

The Masterclasses

The people that attended our expert talks loved them, but when we launched we were only running them at our Sydney office (therefore probably only appealing to people within a 6km radius). So how could we take this offering to a more geographically-diverse audience?

The Culture

How could I flip the mindset of my team, and myself, so that we felt grateful, inspired and lucky to work for a brand that was, literally, changing people's lives?

I also had multiple waves of staff changes. The first lot of staff losses happened in November, 2016. The second wave were not resignations, but redundancies, which happened in the middle of 2017.

Although every loss was tough, it was also the best thing that could have happened in a sense, because I was forced to get on the phones and sell myself. It often pays to get 'close to the ground' of your business again. And what I realised was that people were absolutely in love with our brand and were willing to connect with our audience, engage with us and spend (also that a phone call is a LOT more powerful than an email for getting a quick and positive response from a client).

This time Damian gave me very specific day-by-day targets for six weeks. It was quite incredible – not having worked for anyone for more than 16 years, I relished in having direction to tame my wild brain. I loved having something to work towards; I smashed every goal. The exact same thing happened during my first round of staff losses when, a week before Christmas – traditionally the quietest time of the year according to sales experts – I locked up AU$735,000 of deals, in five days.

After arriving back in the office on January 3, within two weeks we had amassed a further AU$365,000, taking us up to a whopping AU$1.1 million in a matter of weeks. It was hard work, but also the MOST fun I'd had in a long time. I was back on the floor and back in start-up mode again – big time. By far my favourite and most productive place to be.

When *Collective Hub* first launched, I was intimately involved in all sales deals but, as is often the way, as the brand grew so quickly, I'd lost touch with this side of the business – despite how vital it is for our survival. When my remaining staff saw me, joyfully, getting stuck into the action, their morale seemed to rise, too. Despite a VERY tough time of layoffs and resignations, our morale actually seemed better than ever afterwards. We were leaner, more focused and more determined than ever.

On the day that many good people lost their jobs, I sent an email to my team. *"Today was tough and you were all absolutely beyond amazing,"* it read. *"I cannot thank every single one of you enough for your love, loyalty and resilience. You are all incredible and today melted me in ways I could never ever have imagined. It was a hard day for all of us. But every single one, bar none, who either left or stayed, showed up in ways I have never before experienced. Everyone should be very very proud as individuals and as a team. Tomorrow we start to rebuild stronger than ever as a family. I feel so close to all of you and look forward to a positive, big, beautiful, bright future together doing what we set out to do every single day – Ignite Human Potential."*

I could cry, even now, as I read this. It fills my heart with gratitude for my staff, advisers and loyal supporters. I'm also incredibly grateful for the courage I had to shrink down, rethink and rebuild gently. Because I know, without doubt, that if we'd continued to expand in that unconscious, monstrous way, *Collective Hub* could not have continued. And furthermore, I would not have had the insights or courage to make my final decision with regard to the ultimate pivot for the business and this next iteration of my life.

As I write this, my team's morale has never been better. There are only a handful of us working from a co-working space, still in the heart of Sydney, but far, far smaller than our penthouse palace. My team has a renewed energy. Because we cut our salary outgoings we're able to tap into an incredible pool of talented freelancers and contributors that support them, and keep content fresh and relevant. Currently, my editor Amy works remotely from the seaside town of Kiama, two hour's drive away, and rarely comes into the office. Yet, our communication lines have never been more open or efficient.

By scaling down, I was able to refocus on our mission – *Collective Hub* exists to ignite human potential. Really, that's as simple or complex as it goes. And, for the sake of a sustainable business, I chose simple. You can think big, but act small. In fact, it's the most powerful combination available.

As I complete the final edit of this book, I have just reached an entirely new level of shrinkage with no full-time staff or office, only a group of incredible freelancers and my computer. But, that's a topic for another chapter (and another book). Watch this space!

How to shrink-BIG!

1. Focus on the good. I would argue that there is only so much chopping you can do. After you've downsized anything that obviously isn't serving you, rather than focusing on the negatives, focus on the positive elements of your business that you know are profitable (or have the potential to be). Then look for ways to make those departments (or projects) more efficient.

2. Know when to stop. When you've slimmed down so much you suddenly realise you don't even have a designer (this happened to us in April, 2017), you know it's time to stop. When you're slimming, make sure you still have the 'nutrients' you need to produce a quality product, or a decentralised team of amazing freelancers you can rely on.

3. See the positives. And explain these to your team clearly. As I told my staff, a profitable business gives us the chance to make measured decisions about the future, and really focus on what our community and our advertisers want. An unprofitable business doesn't give us that luxury, so we need to make some changes immediately.

4. Hit the trifecta. Instead of trying to change everything, focus on three very specific immediate priorities. For us, it was hitting sponsorship targets for our Kick. Start. Smart. event, increasing sales for our next print edition and increasing ticket sales for Masterclasses. By focusing on three targets, we were able to hit them.

5. Remember your customer. One danger of expanding (or shrinking) too fast is a reduction in customer service. This was brought home to me when we no longer had anyone to answer our reception phone. "But we have an answering machine," argued one of my team. That's not cool when we're a global brand all about communication and interaction.

6. Make the tough call, quickly. When you decide to scale down, take some action immediately. As an entrepreneurial friend who'd also been in this situation told me: "This downsizing really hurt – a couple of people were let go and a number of longtime employees were not happy about having to shift to a new area and they soon quit. Looking back, I wish I'd made this tough call even earlier, but such is life."

@LISAMESSENGER

Think BIG,
act SMALL.
Work smarter
not HARDER.
Fall in love with
YOUR life
AGAIN

BETTER BEFORE BIGGER

The BIGGEST *years in business can be the* TOUGHEST. *Daniel Flynn, co-founder and MD of social enterprise,* THANKYOU *(and dear friend of Collective Hub),* SHARES *his learnings…*

"What's next?" is the one question I get asked the most. Earlier this year I was on the phone to a journalist who asked this question and I said, "Get ready for it… the next big thing at Thankyou is… operational excellence."

It's not quite as exciting as a new product launch or a new country launch… Or is it?

Financial year 2017 was a defining year for Thankyou. We went through growing pains as we experienced the next stage of growth, while also challenging the empires of some of the world's biggest multinationals. We launched our online store, launched an innovation-led nappy range, grew bodycare sales by 44.43 per cent and shipped 2516 truckloads of product across the nation.

But growing pains also led us to champion three words this year: **Better Before Bigger.**

Here are some of our challenging, humbling, stop-doing-cartwheels-around-the-office learnings:

LAUNCHING THANKYOU BABY TOOK DOUBLE THE TIME (AND COST) THAN WE FORECASTED

It's common when launching into a new market to have to invest more than initially planned, and to refine our nappies and stay on-shelf, we had to do just that. It sets us up for future profit wins, but as with all business investments, ultimately it hit this year's bottom line. Mentors have always told me to double the cost and the time of what you think something will take… mentors are usually right.

WE LOST SHELF SPACE IN STORE

In 12 months we lost 47 per cent of ranging for our food and water range. For water, the category has become heavily commoditised (some days you can buy a 24-pack of water on special cheaper than we can make it). This, paired with retailers introducing their private label brands, led to our sales and shelf space decline. We'll unpack the food realities a little further down.

WE GOT CAUGHT UP IN THE WAITING GAME

We had insight that a retailer was going to take our new product range, but in the process it got delayed, delayed and delayed. We set up a team to manage the new business, but the deal landed later than we anticipated. Looking back, it was a short-term problem that has now ironed itself out, but was still challenging for us.

WE GREW RAPIDLY, BUT SOME OF OUR SYSTEMS AND STRUCTURE DIDN'T GROW QUICK ENOUGH

It's classic growing pains, say all the books, but it really hit hard this year. We'd delayed some major system overhauls due to budgets (one system costing hundreds of thousands of dollars). With hindsight, we should have invested earlier.

WE INVESTED IN AN IDEA THAT DIDN'T GO TO PLAN

We acquired an online magazine for parents and rebranded it to an online community and marketing platform to sell advertising, and use the profit to join our nappies and baby care to fund safe births and healthcare... and it didn't work. We rebranded the social media channels to @thankyoubabyaus, and not only gained a ton of valuable lessons but now have our own community of more than 50,000 parents!

THE BOTTOM LINE:

We gave AU$853,458.80 to help end global poverty in FY17. While it's a good result, it's lower than what we had hoped. But considering the tough year and multiple storms we faced, it's a result we can be proud of. It means we've increased our total funding to AU$5.5 million to date! And helped more than 755,338 people get access to a safe birth, healthcare, water and sanitation services and food aid.

THE SOLUTION:

The year was one of refinement, asking hard questions and discovering there are no easy answers. We appointed a Chief Operating Officer, invested in new processes and systems, restructured the team and hired for new roles.

We also made the big call to pull out of one of our four categories (water, food, body care, nappies and baby care). Losing our food range was one of the toughest calls we've made at Thankyou. But we made it for an important reason: focus. Our biggest issue in FY17 was that we lost it.

'Better Before Bigger' meant we called out average products that were draining resources and profit to focus on our core business – to be the best product company, period. There's a wise saying that goes anything is possible... but not everything.

HAPPINESS
is about mindset.
Create from joy.
Then, ANYTHING
is POSSIBLE

Living loudly with less

July, 2017. I just got home to my teeny tiny little happy home in the same clothes I've been wearing on rotation for almost a week (a pair of my partner's boxer shorts – I kid you not – and his t-shirt because I've been too busy to get back here). After moving from my spacious rental into a tiny apartment, most of my furniture is now in Collective Hub's office, because I had absolutely no room to keep it here.

If I'm honest, I'd been dreading moving into this apartment. Recently, there's been so much change and SO much flux that it felt like the final nail in the coffin. The night I moved here from my big spacious airy apartment – after finally finding the courage to face it at 6pm on a Friday night with my PA to support me – I was terrified that it would tip me over the edge into despair.

I think after such a crazy discombobulated week, I was just fearful of what my next stage of life would present. With my home being my sanctuary – my special place of quiet and respite from the world – I was living in fear and trepidation that I would no longer have a sanctuary or a place that felt like home.

But quite the opposite was the case… As I sat in my living room with hardly any furniture and minimal possessions. (Thanks to a purge a few weeks earlier, where I'd been inspired by an interview we did with The Minimalists to give away six bags of my clothing and belongings, and then an item a day for 30 days). I felt an incredible sense of calm and relief wash over me. I hadn't felt this safe and secure in weeks, certainly not in my far more glamorous apartment.

So much so – and here's the kicker – that I wondered why I hadn't thought to live here in all my seven house moves over the past nine years since buying this place. Not once! I had always, I'm ashamed to admit, slightly looked down on this investment which was perfectly nice but not wow-worthy. How silly I was in hindsight when it was exactly what I needed in this moment – comforting, warm, safe and 'real' – all traits that I value so highly.

I have written about my lack of materialism a lot – how I'm the editor who doesn't care for freebies, fashion shows, designer handbags or fast cars. I'd swap it all for a genuine connection with another human, a jog along the seafront or a $6 green smoothie. I've talked in the past about my lack of sentimentality around most possessions – aside from photographs and special keepsakes. But I've never felt more grateful than the weekend I downsized my personal life, and began to scale down my business in unison.

The truth is this: when I'm happy in my life, it actually doesn't matter at all where I live. In fact, I'm happiest, it turns out, in a very small place that I own – unencumbered from grumpy bullying landlords that I've dealt with for the past few years. Here's the thing: if we allow ourselves, suddenly the things we thought imperfect and annoying are actually bliss. And, the things we thought were vital to our happiness suddenly don't matter anymore.

The huge team you thought you needed, the grand office that seemed so vital, the giant meeting room you needed to impress visitors, the latest outfits you needed to look the part… At the end of the day, these don't really have any real impact on the health of your company or your personal happiness.

I say this as someone in the public eye (eugh, I hate that phrase!), who every so often is snapped at events by photographers. Now, I have perhaps something like 40 items of clothing in total. It seems disproportionate for an 'editor', however it is the simple things in life that are the most magical to me, and that help me to achieve my purpose.

So, here I am – being schooled by the universe again! After a period in which my mission for 'moreness' (more staff, more resources, more space) nearly broke us, I'm being forced to remember the gentle healing power of simplicity. I just went to the supermarket and bought four lights for $6 each (bargain!) and now I'm going to have macaroni cheese for my dinner. The glamorous life of a magazine editor? Perhaps not. But a happy life, nonetheless.

Chapter
Four

Diversify, divide
& conquer

CHAPTER FOUR

Diversify, divide & conquer

One of the survival strategies I employed to pull *Collective Hub* back from the brink was to diversify. It might sound counterproductive – building the brand by increasing our strategic partnerships, while we were also trying to slim and scale the business down in other ways – but both strategies do complement each other.

If we could diversify by working with more (carefully chosen!) partners, which is something we've always loved to do at *Collective Hub*, then it would actually lessen the risk for us, because we could share resources, combine our customer bases and boost our reach, considerably.

If we could work with partners we trusted who shared similar vision, values and audience profile – enough so I could strike a deal, then step back from it – it would also free my mind up to work on the wider vision of the company. Which, as a big-picture thinker, is where I get into my 'genius zone' (I have dedicated an entire chapter to this later).

The power of diversification and strategic partnerships has, for a long time, been employed by incredible entrepreneurs and visionaries. Take Sir Richard Branson, who has more than 60 'Virgin' branded companies. But how many of them are actually overseen by the big man himself, and how many are licensing deals?

Because the businessman's brand name carries such weight, he has unlimited partnership opportunities to choose from – and they're incredibly profitable. According to a 2013 report, the keeper of the Virgin brand had at that point made more money in royalties from Virgin Australia than the airline had earned in profits since their 2003 licensing agreement.

In the 10 years through to June, 2013, Branson's company charged about AU$103.1 million (US$82 million) in licensing fees to Brisbane-based Virgin Australia, according to analysis by Bloomberg. Meanwhile, Virgin Australia itself certainly didn't make this much profit. Yet the airline had benefited from the "halo effect of Virgin globally, which... money can't buy," said Virgin Australia's Chief Executive Officer, John Borghetti.

Few of the Virgin brands are wholly owned by the brand's creator himself. Instead, they're run on a day to day basis by companies with a passion for a particular industry. These include Virgin Mobile USA, Virgin Mobile Australia, Virgin Radio and Virgin Music (now part of EMI). In exchange, he receives annual or triennial fees and the brand name becomes bigger and better.

Even Virgin Cola, one of the brand's extensions that infamously failed, is still available in countries including Nigeria and the Philippines, via licensing deals with third parties (showing the power of strategic partnerships in other countries, even if a particular product isn't a fit for your local market).

As *Collective Hub* readers know, I'm lucky enough to know Sir Richard personally (on one memorable occasion he donned a mermaid costume for World Oceans Day. I was lucky enough to find myself helping him get into the costume, and he then used me to balance on as we plopped him in the pool). I remember asking him at one of our catch-ups just how many Virgin companies there were now. And he absolutely did not know! Some people might see this as a bad thing, but I think it's a sign of an incredibly powerful and consistent brand. It is a WONDERFUL thing when you have such a strong brand identity that you can literally do just about anything, transverse any industry and create countless avenues for expansion.

This is exactly in line with my vision. It's always been a part of my longer term plan to build the *Collective Hub* brand and then have a number of different partnerships in place, with sponsorship and licensing deals, to grow the brand even further, but lessen the risk and let the experts do what they do best.

For me, year four felt like the perfect time to push this strategy and put some of the plans I'd had since our launch into action. It can be a slow-burner. You do need a bit of a name first, to make collaboration appealing. It's a lot harder to convince potential partners to collaborate with a fledgling company that no one has ever heard of (although, it's not impossible to convince them!).

So, I sent my incredible partnership manager an email at a ridiculously early time of the morning, when inspiration suddenly struck me and I jumped into action. It read:

"I'm so pumped about this year! As per our discussions, can you please start to put together a list of our 'ideal' strategic partners in a number of spaces. Basically, as you know, these are some areas that we have identified as potential growth areas but we don't necessarily want to take on the risk or resourcing. I am keen, along with you, to meet with a number of them over the next few weeks to discuss bigger commercial partnerships and see where it lands us."

In the email, I divided our possible growth areas into a variety of exciting, varied categories: design (including web and possibly an app), content, co-working spaces, events, online, corporate alignment, and other media alignment. From there, we could look at ways to align ourselves to other people, license our name smartly and collaborate authentically. What could they do for us... and what could we do for them?

Scratch our back...

've written in my previous books and talked in our Masterclasses about the importance of forming partnerships that are mutually beneficial. This isn't about sucking from someone else's resources – it's about building an empowering partnership for both parties who can truly benefit from working together.

At *Collective Hub* we have a LOT to offer. Whenever we partner with brands, especially for 'real world' events where they get to interact with our readers, they are blown away by the passion, engagement and commitment of our community to support everything we do, get behind meaningful causes and, of course, buy our products. That, in itself, is invaluable. We actually have to turn down a lot of event and launch offers from venues and brands who want to collaborate, because there aren't enough hours in the week to plan them and attend them. (And I like to get to as many *Collective Hub* events as possible, because I truly LOVE meeting you all).

Our content is also king, to borrow one of Bill Gates' favourite phrases. We produce hundreds of articles a month across online and print, tapping into the knowledge of *Collective Hub*'s experts and connections. In an age where brands need unlimited content to share across their online channels, exploring content-sharing opportunities – for a price or mutual contra exchange – was also an exciting avenue. I shared some of the secrets of my collaboration strategies in my book *Money & Mindfulness* (head to collectivehub.com if you want to find out more).

One of the top strategies is to leverage anything! In all my books I talk about the importance of value exchange because it is so important. What do you have to offer that's non-monetary? In this day and age, it's all about attention. How can you boost someone else's profile using your product or service, and how can this be leveraged to convince them to build a partnership? 'Value exchange' are the two most important words we have lived by in growing our brand.

As I first shared in *Daring & Disruptive*, I've always been a deal broker. It's one of my favourite things to do, almost more than anything else. I just love connecting people, and I love creating and facilitating value exchange. I don't use those words lightly or by accident – they are used with extreme purpose because they seem to represent a concept that people have the most difficulty coming to terms with.

Before I started my first company in 2001, I worked for a sponsorship agency where my entire job was to broker deals. I had a great deal of respect for my boss at the time, but I remember vividly that I had him constantly rolling his eyes, as I kept banging on and on about 'strategic alliances'. The truth is, regardless of what job, industry or market you are in, we all need to be able to build relationships and ultimately sell.

Need inspiration? There are incredible case studies out there, showing the power of 'co-branding' a product or experience. Who can forget when GoPro and Red Bull teamed up for 'Stratos', in which American skydiver and daredevil Felix Baumgartner jumped from a helium balloon more than 38km (24 miles) above the earth's surface (with a GoPro strapped to his chest to capture every moment)? Not only did Baumgartner set three world records that day, but the 'full story' footage has been watched by more than 19 million people since. It's the epitome of perfect brand alignment.

There are many more brilliant examples. My ABSOLUTE favourite example of all time was when the search engine Bing collaborated with Jay-Z for the launch of his book *Decoded*. They left actual pages of the book in locations across the globe and posted virtual pages on Bing Maps. I've watched the accompanying YouTube clip hundreds of times.

After launching their smart watch, Apple partnered with luxe fashion brand Hermès to create a high-fashion version, describing it as, "the culmination of a partnership based on parallel thinking, singular vision and mutual regard."

At the more attainable end of the fashion scale, high-street brand H&M have created crowd-pulling sell-out lines with more high-calibre brands including Karl Lagerfeld, Erdem and Roberto Cavalli. In the US, Target have had similar success with designer collaborations, creating limited-edition lines with 3.1 Phillip Lim, Zac Posen and Missoni (who we profiled in issue 51 of *Collective Hub*).

Making a mark in different industries, Starbucks has partnered with Spotify, McDonald's regularly partners with Monopoly, and Victoria's Secret has joined forces with the NFL on a range of sports-inspired underwear.

After Lego saw net profits rise in 2015 by 31 per cent to US$1.34 billion, they credited much of their record growth to specialist product lines like the Lego Star Wars line. This was then developed into an animated series, Lego Star Wars: The Freemaker Adventures, produced by Disney XD. "The series is a great testament to our longstanding and successful partnership with Lucasfilm and Disney," said Jill Wilfert, vice president of licensing and entertainment at the Lego Group.

The list goes on and on and the potentials are endless if you have faith in your brand, in your name and in your influence. Especially if you're willing to think outside the box when it comes to limitless possibilities.

For us, one of the most exciting partnerships to date was our Graduate Certificate in Collective Entrepreneurship in conjunction with Torrens University Australia. Together, we created a course like no other, based on hands-on, collaborative learning and industry immersion.

Part of my purpose has always been to educate, inspire and ignite the potential of our community, many of whom have entrepreneurial ambitions. So, this seemed like a perfect partnership – and it has been.

However, it was also a LONG time in the making (nearly two years!) and an important lesson in patience and conscious pickiness. We were wooed quite seriously by seven different possible partners, all in the education field, before connecting with Torrens. With every offer, the deals got sweeter and sweeter. But I always had a deep, gut instinct that a perfect opportunity would arise, when the timing was right and the partner was perfect.

Now I look back often at what partnerships we could have entered into and shudder at the thought. Although I'm grateful for the other institutions' interest, they weren't a good fit for us. We would have created a 'good' product, but it wouldn't have been exceptional – or life-changing for participants.

Instead, we met (and fell in love with) Torrens, which is part of the Laureate International Universities network, with 80 universities across 29 countries, and resources for a MASSIVE build. Working with them has been a joy and an education. And, hearing the stories of students who have gone on to launch successful brands thanks to what they learnt, makes my heart want to explode with pride and gratitude.

Diversification also allowed us to undo the damage of the extortionate rent we were paying on our office. In addition to launching a co-working space, I realised the outdoor area was the perfect spot to hold events. But there are only so many events my slimmed-down team could manage.

So, rather than trying to do it all ourselves, we reached out to companies with incredible experiences in different event categories. Would they like to run co-branded events in our space and tap into our community? Before I knew it, our office had become an after-hours hive of activity. Along with workplace wellness consultants, Wellineux, we held evenings of mindfulness, qigong and stress reduction.

We've also held events in our office with the amazing wedding and event caterers Gallivant. We decided that our expertise was not necessarily in running and hosting events on our own deck and that it would detract

RISK & RESILIENCE

from our focus – so why not outsource to the experts so we wouldn't have to worry about logistics, licenses, security and catering, and just clip the ticket on the way through. We had a great deck. They had a great client base. Win-win for everyone!

We also hosted mentoring sessions for one of our fabulous clients Lexus, when we collaborated on a Start Up Package in conjunction with them. We let some of the winners of their competition use our office to do their own pop-ups. Incredibly, some of the fledgling brands I mentored have now gone onto huge things. I received an email from one founder the other day who has just been accepted onto the Chobani Incubator program and been awarded a private label contract with Aldi. Proof that smart collaborations aren't only beneficial for the two brands involved, but can also empower your community.

There were also our Masterclasses (we held 62 live, face-to-face ones in that office in six months), which brought together experts across business, branding, marketing, licensing and content creation, to hosts talks on their specialist subjects ('Protect your business, legally' and 'Learn to love your money'). In addition to asking our favourite people to take to the 'stage', we also teamed up with book publishers, global brands and television production companies. We provided the venue and the audience, and they provided the talent.

I have to be honest here. Although the above partnerships were seamless, some were far more testing. We had issues with partners not representing us accurately on marketing material (honestly, at least get our name right!). I quickly learnt to make sure we approved all publicity material.

Lesson two: always make sure you get every promise in writing. We've worked with strategic partners on magazine covers who simply didn't stick to their end of the bargain. There was one high-profile blogger who I was pumped to feature on our cover, not only because I knew our readers would learn a lot from her journey, but also because she had a HUGE social media following which could elevate our reach globally.

After promising to share the issue across her channels, we got nothing – not a tweet! We knew she was overjoyed with the article, because she told us so. But when we politely emailed her people, asking when we could expect a cover share we got no response. Twelve weeks later, when the magazine was no longer on sale in shops, she finally posted about it (you could still back-order the issue from our website but we'd missed the optimum sales window).

You win some, you lose some. And, you can't hold resentment for the plans that don't quite materialise or work out in the way you hoped they would. When it comes to strategic partnerships, you also have to learn to adjust your expectations. When I'm sitting in a meeting with a prospective partner, my brain goes into overdrive. It's the kind of person I am! 'Let's do this, let's do that, lets send a rocket to the moon!' I'm a BIG thinker, so it's easy to get very carried away with ideas and possibilities. But, sometimes you have to start smaller with collaborations that are achievable and then plan a long-term strategy for the bigger stuff.

In 2017, one of my highlights was shooting Jamie Oliver for our cover. Since the dawn of the Naked Chef's career I've been enamoured with his branding, especially since he moved into food activism, on a mission to help children eat healthier. This collaboration has been another long-term project, involving countless emails, false starts and clashing schedules (Jamie O is a busy, busy person!).

Finally, it happened… And the entrepreneur and founder of Ministry of Food was just as authentic, down to earth and endearingly honest as I imagined. Jamie admitted, while we sat chatting in hair and makeup, that his foodie magazine was not turning a profit (it closed less than six months later). We also talked about all sorts of other big issues in the world that needed tackling and I wanted to shout, 'lets tackle this together'. But my baby still needed a lot of care and focus and at that time I also didn't want to distract from the reason for our meeting: to create exclusive content for *Collective Hub* and our online channels that would educate and inspire our community. So, I bit my tongue and postponed that possible partnership for later. Sometimes you have to focus and trust that, if it's meant to, a bigger collaboration will unfold in its own space and time.

Be patient.
Your perfect
(creative) partner
is coming...

Throw me to the Wolves and I'll come back leading the pack!

Uniting = ~~uplifting~~

Diversification wasn't only good for our revenue. It also gave me, and therefore my team, a morale boost just when we needed it. It's wonderful to sit in meetings and hear just how excited incredible companies are about working with you. I love the perspective a new partner can bring, and the fruitful projects that can be born from listening to someone else's opinion.

I emerged from one meeting with the CEO of a digital lifestyle magazine so exhilarated. At the time, the independent publication got more than 1.2 million unique views a month (astounding for a relatively new launch), produced a lot of video content and were interested in launching a print magazine, too. They suggested that, alongside a few other independent media companies, we look into content sharing and cross promotion. Since then we've shared content with News.com.au and The Huffington Post. I loved that, rather than seeing each other as 'the enemy', a new wave of media organisations could see the power of working together.

Many of these partnerships also took me out of the office on trips and excursions, which allowed my team to work autonomously and also gave me distance and perspective. As I've discovered, it's not healthy to hover over your staff, especially in times of crisis when they're already a little edgy.

In May, 2017 I stood in the Yarra Valley, in the most beautiful part of Victoria. For the second year in a row, I was there to host a co-branded event with a vineyard. I stood in this incredible location, surrounded by incredible diners, enjoying an amazing three-course meal. All I could think was, 'Wow, people pay a fortune to hold their weddings, birthdays and corporate events here.'

Yet, someone else pays us a LOT of money to co-brand this event. They organise all the styling, the food and the drinks, then we receive a portion of the ticket sale revenue. It's also one of the most fun events on my calendar, which I genuinely look forward to. Business deals aside, I'm now dear friends with the owners of the vineyard and love spending time with them. In that moment, I felt incredibly blessed to have that opportunity. It seemed extraordinary.

And still, I am doing deals and still people are loving us. As I write this, we're probably close to more than 200 events since launch and every day we get requests for more. Despite losing inordinate amounts of money, it was an important reminder – we STILL should be so damn proud of what we've created – a big, bold brand that so many people adore. Yay us!

When you diversify smartly, with help, support and third parties, suddenly the impossible seems possible and the unmanageable is achievable. It shouldn't be surprising, really, that the answer to building a sustainable business lies in sharing. Thanks to Airbnb and Uber, we share our homes, we share our cars and we share our skills through platforms such as Fiverr. Why not share your brand name – or at least lend it out – to a company who can use it to do great things, and reach whole new heights?

BUT it was becoming clear that, even in this area of our business, our model needed tweaking, and our behind-the-scenes processes needed to be adjusted. When you're holding sell-out events attended by hundreds of people and STILL not turning a profit, you need to examine the back-end of your production. So I did…

10 tips from a start-up survivor

1. Small teams can be powerful. At our smallest size, we were able to be the most nimble and flexible, which is so important within an ever-changing market. A smaller team also freed up resources to hire incredible specialists on a project-per-project basis.

2. Making people redundant is horrible, but that horror s short-lived when you realise your brand still functions perfectly without them. t also helps when the people you're making redundant agree they were never a good match for your brand in the first place and leave amicably.

3. Sit with your team and be a great motivator. When I moved out of a 'corner' office and rejoined my people at one desk, my team's energy and enthusiasm went off the charts overnight – and I felt happier, too.

4. Gamify everything, from ad sales to your team's fitness goals. Coloured charts on the walls, which showed our sales progress, made everyone excited to see sales rise. We even began a competition to see who could log the most steps on our Fitbits.

5. Never trust banks – they will sink you in a heartbeat.

6. Know your data intimately.

7. Relationships are everything, especially when it comes to sales and partnerships.

8. There's a limit to contra. Someone offered me a year's supply of fluorescent sandals in return for an ad. It seems they had taken my 'there are more currencies than cash' mantra quite seriously. Learn to say no somet mes. You can't pay bills with free footwear.

9. Your self-belief is the MOST important asset you have.

10. Anything is possible, even at your lowest point.

@LISAMESSENGER

Chapter Five

Keeping your
soul business

CHAPTER FIVE
Keeping your soul business

There is a danger to cutting, splicing and diversifying your business, especially when you start to bring in advisers as I did, some of them from a corporate background with invaluable – but slightly more traditional – knowledge of big business. The worry is that you lose the essence of the rebellious, disruptive and unique model that made your brand different in the first place.

As I've said in the past, when *Collective Hub* launched, none of my team, including me, had any experience in the magazine game and, though it was tough, it worked in our favour. Those first few years were definitely the most fun of the entire five years. But in year four, after our spate of redundancies and evacuations, I did begin to hire some more traditional people and, as a result I felt us morphing into a more traditional media brand, playing by the rules. That is not me at all!

Take our cover design. There are a lot of unwritten rules in the old-school magazine world about what a cover needs to sell – it must be a famous person everyone instantly recognises, they must have strong eye contact looking straight down the barrel of the camera, no children and no animals. It must be a never-before-seen, exclusive shot. You shouldn't use green… blah blah blah and on it goes. Yawn. There are some other racially and totally politically incorrect ones that I have heard, which nearly made me physically ill. But let's not go there!! Historically, some of *Collective Hub*'s best-selling covers have broken every rule in the book.

One of my favourite ever covers is the infamous issue 23. I had a VERY well-known celebrity on the cover, which ticked every aforementioned box.

However, something just didn't feel right. I didn't want to conform. I was sick of the rules. So after we had already gone to print (there is a 24-hour window we have from when we go to print until the printer lands the 'proofs' with us. In this window, I was getting agitated – so much so that I said to my art director, "Humour me – find me a woman's back." This was a gut feel. And it was strong. It wasn't pre-thought-out, but it just came out of my mouth. It felt rebellious. It felt right. It was my money. My magazine. I was ready to take a risk.

My team had already interviewed the incredible travel bloggers Murad Osmann and his wife, Natalia Zakharova, and we had a picture that had already been seen on Instagram, so it was not original. It BROKE EVERY RULE. I've written about this many times and it's well-documented about how I stripped out the cover story and left it blank for our readers and wrote a simple cover line, "Be the story that must be told." It went OFF!!

Another sell-out featured huge, colourful flamingos. And another, the beyond fabulous Iris Apfel, who was 94 at the time and had only stepped into her purpose in her mid-eighties. I love that our readers are drawn to such high-impact images and make up their own minds about which pictures appeal to them while standing in a shop.

Which is why I was so upset to suddenly find myself in meetings on one end of conversations about how we needed a new cover strategy. "We can't do that. It won't sell," was uttered about covers that didn't conform to traditional guidelines.

This hurts and it's hard. Because one of the ways we built such a frickin kick-arse brand in the first place was by being rebellious, not giving a f*ck and not knowing the rules, so we could break every single one of them – mostly unintentionally, but also very intentionally to buck the status quo.

It came to a head when I went into a meeting with our team and discovered the freelance art director, who had been hired by one of our advisers, didn't even

know who I was. She clearly had no idea about the history of *Collective Hub*, who started the company or why. This isn't about me wanting to be famous (at all!). It's about wanting staff members who are invested in our brand, know why it exists and what we're aiming to achieve with our purpose. And this wasn't just happening to us. I can't tell you the number of people we interview and ask about the founder or start-up story – and they have no idea…

On the flip side, you can hire people who love the brand TOO MUCH. Recently, my amazing marketing director left to go on maternity leave after nine and a half years working with me, across my different start-ups. Before she left, we had an amazingly frank conversation about what she thought went wrong in our toughest times. Why did our culture go from so contented to so disconnected? She believed that we hired too many 'fangirls', who adored the magazine and liked every social media post we put up.

That's a good thing, right? The problem is they joined *Collective Hub* with the expectation that it would be one big, glamorous press trip. The hard work, long hours and often boring, repetitive jobs that are involved in working for a multi-channel publication, didn't always match their filtered view of the magazine world. This quickly led to discontentment and the 'we want more' attitude I had to battle.

My remaining, core team were more excited and invested in the future of *Collective Hub* than ever, but it was a stark reminder that I had to be protective of the people I allowed into our culture – even if they were only in the office for a day. The advisory board we enlisted, the freelancers we hired, the partners we worked with and even the interns who sporadically joined us – they would all, in a small or large way, influence our future.

I didn't want *Collective Hub* to survive if we lost the heart and soul of the business, which was our point of difference in the first place. One of the risks of losing the essence of your brand is that, as an entrepreneur, you begin to lose the love of what you created. With every meeting about what we 'should' do, and every email from a complaining staff member, I began to pull away and become less connected to the company that was my baby.

I've often heard founders say, 'They are great start-up people. They are not great CEOs.' This could definitely be true for me. I love the buzz of creating, of rebelling, of moving forward. I can't stand the minutiae, the operations, the systems and the processes. I know that now, 100 per cent, and I'm very grateful for these lessons. I'd never been in a high growth start-up and so, like so many of us, was charting the waters as I went. There is much I would do differently now. That's not to say I have any regrets at all. Not one. I know I am absolutely destined to be an entrepreneur my entire life – so I will be part of many, many start-ups in my lifetime. These lessons for me (and I hope you) have been beyond invaluable!

According to a UK study, 35 per cent of entrepreneurs lose motivation to run their business, at least once a year. The report by British accountancy firm Haines Watts found that money worries is one of the largest contributors, alongside the volume of work, responsibility to their staff and an uneven work-life balance.

It can be hard to stay focused, especially when everything around you feels like it's changing. A shift in staff, revenue, environment or the feedback loop from your clients or community can also affect your business 'mojo' (the desire, passion or motivation you feel for your company). When people have lost their work passion, it often means they're burnt out or plain bored, according to research from the workplace review website, Glassdoor.

Your customers will also pick up on the shift, when your business begins to lose its soul. You fall in love with a boutique fashion brand, only to find the quality of their clothes slides as they hit mass production. Your favourite café hires new people and their customer service suddenly wanes. You don't get a smile with your coffee. They no longer try to remember your order. It's a small change, but it also matters greatly.

"You've got to find what you love," said Steve Jobs during a commencement speech at Stanford University. "The only way to do great work is to love what you do. If you haven't found it yet, keep looking. Don't settle. As with all matters of the heart, you'll know when you find it." For the Apple founder, this wasn't about building technology – it was about giving normal people the means to unleash their creativity through gadgetry.

Since his death, some people have criticised Apple for losing its soul – overpricing products and bringing new ones out too quickly. An article in *Fortune* magazine asked, 'Has Apple lost its design mojo?', after customers complained about fraying cables and unintuitive software. I personally don't agree with the naysayers. When you run a global company that has sold 78 million iPhones in a quarter, it's impossible to please everyone.

But even the fact Apple's ethos is being debated is enough to show how important it is to be true to your spirit. If you do change the culture, ethos or direction of your company, it isn't a bad thing, but do it consciously for the betterment of your staff and your customers. Because you might have to defend your decision when the changes set in.

We asked...

JAMIE OLIVER

Jamie Oliver, food activist and founder of the Ministry of Food has created an edible empire. But, with the closure of multiple restaurants and his namesake magazine, he's also not immune to challenges.

HOW DO YOU MAINTAIN FOCUS?

"There's only a certain amount of time, and I have a big family. I think ultimately there's only so much time. We dedicate a lot of that to filming and producing content, which becomes the film for that year and maybe ripples on to the next year. Everything else riffs from that. We try to put purpose into everything we do. We're all about raising the bar. Some of the most important stuff I do right now is with big organisations – some controversial ones – and I have to make a call. Sometimes my team make a call and I override it. [In] the food industry, some of the most powerful things I've done is working with the enemy. But the world is changing – CEOs are changing, politics is changing. I guess, having a longer view is the really meaningful thing."

Clear your vision

In January, 2017, after Phase One of *Collective Hub*'s most momentous changes I sat down with two of my senior staff members and spent some time re-working our vision. It took an entire day to put together, with much to-ing and fro-ing, word play, laughter and debates about the best way to word it. In the (lengthy!) deck that we eventually created, we outlined the four pillars of our brand.

I felt, very clearly, that with all the stripping, scaling and subtracting we were doing to streamline, strategise and become more sustainable, we had to make sure – more than ever – that we didn't waver from the purpose of *Collective Hub* or, most importantly, give our community a below average product (believe me, they would tell us!).

There have certainly always been things I would NOT compromise on in the past, although some of these have changed over time. Paper quality, for example. Although *Collective Hub* had changed its paper stock since we launched – which DID save us money – I refused to go with the cheapest paper on the market because the look of our magazine is part of the reason people love us.

The same with the venues we hold our events in. No saving is worth holding an event in a space that's dark, gloomy and dimly lit with uncomfortable seating and no open windows. As I've always said, I NEED light and fresh air to feel inspired, and so do most people. That's why my location is so important when planning events and why I would never consider a cut-price venue that didn't have the right vibe.

But, in our current state, we did need to find ways to compromise. That's one of the reasons we decided to go back to publishing bi-monthly instead of monthly, and landed on the even-more-dramatic decision you'll read about in the following chapters, because it wouldn't spread our resources so thin.

My point is, with all these changes, we HAD to be crystal clear about our purpose, ethos and the most important elements of our brand going forward. This is some of the content we included in our re-worked vision deck:

Collective Hub:
OUR FOUR PILLARS

1. F*CK THE RULES
COURAGE, GAME-CHANGING, VISIONARY,
FLIP EVERYTHING, NO BOUNDARIES

2. HONESTY
RELATABLE, RAW, HUMAN, GROUNDED,
STORY BEHIND THE STORY

3. INTELLECT AND STYLE
SMART, INSPIRING, INNOVATIVE, DESIGN, BEAUTY

4. BETTER AS A COLLECTIVE
COLLABORATIVE, SHARED LEARNING,
'LET'S DO IT', CONNECTIONS, SUPPORTING

In that meeting we also identified and summarised our audience in these five avatar descriptions:

THE 'MADE IT' ENTREPRENEUR

A source of inspiration for the entrepreneurial community. They're in a position to give back. Our role is to connect with them and tell the story behind the story in a relatable way.

THE EMERGING ENTREPRENEUR

These are the people who have taken the leap and are on the journey. They're often a source of inspiration to others but are usually under-resourced and are focused on their own agenda. Our role is to share their story, validate their success and help promote their business.

THE SENIOR INTRAPRENEUR

Despite never making the break from corporate life, these are the high performing C-suite execs who are constantly challenging themselves and their teams. Our role is to share our learnings from the entrepreneurial world to help them build high-performing teams and businesses.

THE JUNIOR INTRAPRENEUR

Bright young executives with loads of ambition, they dream of starting their own business one day. Our role is to fill their minds with entrepreneurial inspiration that they can apply to their working life immediately… and that might inspire them to launch a great business in the future.

…AND BETTY

Betty is the girl next door. She doesn't have entrepreneurial parents, an elite education or a wealth inheritance. But she still has big hopes and ambitions. Our role is to tell the stories of real people, with real struggles who rise up and succeed. And to inspire Betty to be the best version of herself.

We also got VERY clear about our new, overarching vision – to become the most influential company in entrepreneurship, business and people performance in the world. This was far wider and more expansive than our mission when we started out as a print magazine ('to ignite human potential'). It's also separate to my personal purpose ('to become an entrepreneur for entrepreneurs'). This is why I have always said since the day we launched, "It's not about the print. It's never been about the print. Be able to morph with the market and pivot!"

Whether you're in year two or year 22 of your company, this is a thought-provoking process I'd recommend every founder go through with their core team often. It's not just about defining what you are, but what you're not, too.

We wrote a list of dos and don'ts for *Collective Hub*'s messaging that we would be able to refer back to while working in EVERY aspect of the business, from creating content to marketing, from promotions to 'real world' events and virtual hangouts...

Collective Hub:

IS STYLISH... ISN'T SUPERFICIAL
IS COURAGEOUS... ISN'T CRAZY
IS VISIONARY... ISN'T PREACHY
IS CONNECTED... ISN'T COCKY
IS INNOVATIVE... ISN'T GIMMICKY
IS INSPIRING... ISN'T INTIMIDATING
IS COLLABORATIVE... ISN'T CLIQUEY
IS INTELLIGENT... ISN'T INTELLECTUAL
IS SHARED LEARNING... ISN'T LECTURING
IS F*CK THE RULES
IS BRUTALLY HONEST
IS BETTER TOGETHER

This re-write was very necessary because we've grown so much since we launched. Our mission needed to encapsulate all of our present products and future avenues – some of which already exist and some of which we hadn't invented yet. Everything we produce exists to inspire and educate people on how to become the best version of themselves so that no human potential goes unrealised. By using the four pillars we'd outlined, I was confident we could achieve this.

Revisiting your mission statement is such a powerful, clarifying and exciting strategy. It helps you remember where you come from and where you want to be heading. In issue 50 of *Collective Hub* – our special anniversary edition – we interviewed the amazing female founder behind the British brand Not on the High Street. The award-winning platform – where small businesses can sell their products – hosts more than 5000 partners, selling more than 200,000 different products. In 2016, its sellers made £158 million in gross sales, with Not on the High Street taking a commission for every transaction. Yet in 2015, its founder Holly Tucker stepped down as CEO of the brand she called her 'second baby' (her first being her son) to start a new venture, Holly & Co, a mentoring agency for small business owners.

"I love business, so running a successful company did work for me," she told us. "But [at Not on the High Street] I wasn't seeing my son – or a single piece of creative leaving the building."

Despite a shift in direction she remembers her roots. In the main office of Holly & Co is the dining table she began her first venture from. It has a plaque on it that reads, 'Not on the High Street was founded on this very table'.

Some amazing entrepreneurs have been amazingly honest about how easy it is to lose your direction if you're not mindful – and the tricks they use to stay on track.

Blake Mycoskie, the founder of social enterprise TOMS – the retailer that donates a pair of shoes to a child in need for every pair sold – says, "Focus on your passion, nothing else matters". The company has expanded from shoes to coffee – with every TOMS Roasting Co. product you purchase, TOMS will help provide safe water to a person in need. It's a divergence from their initial offering, but is still perfectly in line with the company's pillars of 'improving lives' and 'thoughtful partnerships'.

As I discovered, everything – whether it's your culture, product or publicity material – comes down to customers and your community. How can you make them happier, healthier or make their lives easier? This is really, at the end of the day, the key to the world's most successful companies, from Apple to Airbnb, Uber and the incredible med-tech start-ups changing how we care for the sick and dying.

In those few horrendous – and I mean horrendous weeks – of losing money and shedding staff, I was SO worried about what was going on internally. But the really sobering and grounding thought is, as long as our 2.6 million strong community see that we are looking after them, then everything is okay. And so, while we desperately tried to manage the carnage that was going on within our company, it was most important that our community was still happy and we were still being everything we should be to them. Everything is relative and everything has perspective.

With this thought – despite the atrocity of those few weeks and the upheaval of 26 or so staff, I found it in my heart to be grateful that nothing was damaging our brand externally and that, from a community interfacing perspective, everything was just as good (in fact better – after all the brand was still growing at a cracking pace) as it had ever been. Even if, financially, we were still on shaky foundations, our four pillars were keeping us vertical.

Once I rewrote our mission – and began to make every decision based on it – our culture began to flow again. It was really that instantaneous. And I began to see signs and messages everywhere I went – gentle, nudging reminders to stay on our path, despite distraction and outside influence.

In my book, *Purpose* I wrote about the life-changing trip I took to India during one of the busiest growth periods of *Collective Hub*, when I slept at meditation centres, connected with incredible people and embraced the most beautiful self-care rituals (many of which I let slide during our most worrying, struggling period).

After revisiting our mission statement, one night as I sat journaling in my living room, I decided to listen to the dance music I was hooked on during that trip. And, the most INCREDIBLE thing happened. As I wrote in my diary, a song came on my playlist – "Something New" by the band, Faul.

These aren't the exact lyrics of the song, but it's how I heard them in that moment: "What is the purpose of my life my baby? Is my fortune the main act? Are you ready to create something new? I don't want it to be all the same. Let me take you away. Can you see the light? I guess we find our way."

It felt like a gift from the universe and a reminder at the perfect moment. It's okay to shift, pivot and move forward, as long as you're guided by your heart and your gut – not a set of rules that others have written for you.

A CHECK-LIST FOR SOUL BUSINESS

- [ ] ONLY KEEP THOSE WHO BELIEVE IN YOUR VISION.
- [ ] DON'T FIGHT FOR THE ONES WHO LEAVE WHEN THE GOING GETS TOUGH.
- [ ] REWARD ON K.P.I.S, NOT JUST FOR THE HELL OF IT.
- [ ] KNOW YOUR 'WHY' EVERY SINGLE DAY.
- [ ] NURTURE RELATIONSHIPS FROM THE GET GO.
- [ ] KNOW THAT THERE WILL BE DISAPPOINTMENTS.
- [ ] USE THE PAIN TO FUEL YOU.
- [ ] NEVER GET INTO THIS POSITION AGAIN.
- [ ] BE RESILIENT AS F*CK.
- [ ] KNOW THAT THE THINGS THAT FLOORED YOU YESTERDAY WILL BE NOTHING LIKE WHAT'S COMING.
- [ ] ALWAYS BELIEVE SOMETHING WONDERFUL IS ABOUT TO HAPPEN.
- [ ] GET BACK TO START-UP MODE.
- [ ] SLOW DOWN TO SPEED UP.
- [ ] BREATHE.

We asked...

CATHIE REID

Cathie Reid is a co-founder of Icon Group, Australia's fastest growing provider of integrated cancer care services, valued at over AU$1 billion in 2018.

HOW DOES IT FEEL TO NEARLY LOSE A FORTUNE?

"I've never encountered a business owner who hasn't experienced at least one point in their business history where they genuinely wondered if it was possible to survive and come out the other side. [My partner] Stuart and I have worked together for close to 20 years now and we've had our share of hairy moments across that time.

The toughest of these came at a time that will undoubtedly spark memories of similar challenges for others, post the financial crisis that swept the world in 2008. To backtrack a little, by 2007 we'd built a sizeable pharmacy business providing medication management services to the private hospital and aged-care sector across Australia.

Just before Easter, 2007 we got a call from our largest client to say that over the next 18 months as our contracts with their sites expired, they would be taking their pharmacy services in-house as a way of delivering on their shareholder growth requirements. Once the transition was complete, this would remove around 60 per cent of our current revenue and profitability, leaving the business unsustainable. Neither of us had a lot of appetite for chocolate that Easter.

This triggered a fairly focused period of market analysis and strategic thinking, the outcome of which saw us identify two opportunities where we believed our existing IP could be utilised to deliver diversification plays, which would serve the dual purpose of both ensuring sustainability going forward, and reducing the future risk of another customer being able to generate a similar impact.

Each of the identified opportunities was relatively capital intensive which, combined with the borrowings that the business was already carrying, saw us heavily geared by late 2008 when the world's financial markets changed dramatically. It wasn't a great time to be carrying nearly AU\$35 million in debt and barely making interest cover.

By then we had seen a significant proportion of the impact of the lost business, but knew there was still worse to come before either of the new opportunities started contributing to the bottom line.

That began the most stressful period of our business lives. There were many days and nights where we really didn't know if we were going to be able to find a way out the other side, but the knowledge of the consequences of not being able to navigate a path kept us going.

It wasn't the personal consequences – there were definitely times when dealing with those seemed easier than finding the will to keep going – but the impact that the business folding would have on the 300 people who worked for us and their families, and the disruption of care to our patients and health care facility customers.

There was a limit to how much we could share with our team about just how challenging things really were. The fear of what could eventuate was almost paralysing at times, and we were loathe to put that degree of pressure on others around us. Our leadership team knew things were tight, but my brother Andrew, our CFO at the time, was the only one who really knew just how close to the wire it was.

When we reflect on that time, there were two main things that got us through. The first was absolute financial discipline, that saw us build a budget and deliver on it for 36 consecutive months. That didn't generate much confidence when the budget was showing a worsening position as the final contracted sites exited, but once we started heading up the curve again things started to get ever so slightly easier.

The other was the strength we drew from each other. There were nights when I sat sobbing on the couch after the children had gone to bed, wondering how we'd ever find a way, while Stuart held me and told me we'd be okay, and other nights when it was my turn to reassure him of the same.

That period of time has now retreated to being a single slide in the deck we use when telling our business story, but it's one that never fails to summon up memories of undoubtedly the most challenging time I've ever experienced in business, and the greatest lessons I've ever learnt about the value of strategy, focus and a commitment to doing what you say you're going to do.

Icon Group was valued at over AU$1 billion in a transaction in September, 2017 which saw an investment consortium of Goldman Sachs, QIC and Pagoda replace our previous private equity partner Quadrant.

For Stuart and I and the rest of the Icon Group leadership team, it means an increased ability to deliver on our mission of providing the best cancer care possible to as many people as possible, as close to their homes as possible. The connections into Asia that our new investors deliver ensure that we are ideally placed to be able to make a difference to the Asian region's increasing cancer burden, and that excites us far more than numbers on a page.

After revisiting our ~~mission~~ statement, ~~one~~ night as I sat ~~journ~~aling in my living room ~~I~~ decided to listen to the dance ~~music~~ ...

happened ...
came on my ...
~~husband, Paul~~ ...

~~These aren't~~ the exa...
so ... but it's how I ...
moment: "w...
~~safe my baby~~ ...
~~and I've~~ ...
new ...
Let ~~me~~ take ...

~~you~~ ...
rules that c... ers hav...

Not all storms come to disrupt your life.

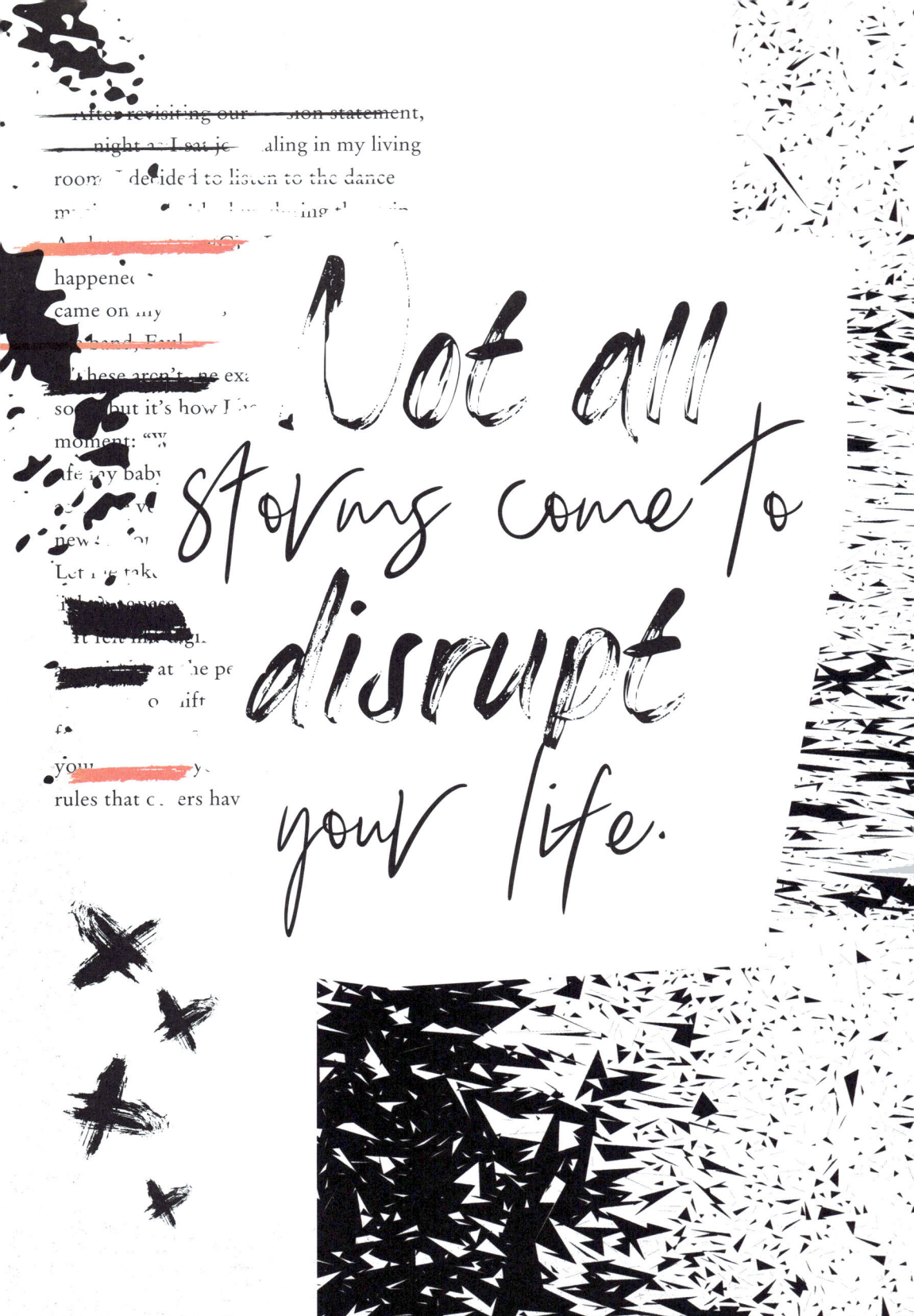

Some come to clear your path.

— ANON

Chapter Six

People & perspective

CHAPTER SIX
People & perspective

In January, 2017 we went from losing AU$150,000 a month to 'only' showing a AU$1200 loss on our balance sheets. The coming March was looking a little dicey, with a projected AU$280,000 loss forecasted, but I still almost had that in my offset account from property sales, so it was doable – just.

We'd made incredible progress by shrinking rapidly and renewing our strategies. There were still mornings when I woke up in a cold sweat (I'm only human after all), but our situation felt far less dire. And, I was quickly learning a very important lesson – as a disruptive entrepreneur in a difficult industry, there will always be people waiting to pull you down. There will always be people who warn you off continuing, constantly!

Interestingly, the people with the biggest, loudest opinions are often the people with the least experience, who've never been in your shoes or experienced what you're going through. If you can surround yourself with good friends and advisers who HAVE done this on a bigger scale before, they have the power to put your situation into perspective.

When self-doubt kicks in, I've never felt more grateful to have confidants who've been there, done that and, in many cases, are still living it. Instead of being shocked by my financial predicament, they made my situation feel normal and, most importantly, survivable.

A dear friend, who has technologically revolutionised a particular sector, came in for a meeting with my consultant and I. She told me about the time she was in debt AU$55 million to a bank and, after a brief downward spiral in business, she had to keep banks and creditors at bay until, thankfully, her finances headed upwards again. Now, her business has a seven-figure valuation. At the time, another friend was waiting on a AU$170 million payout from one of his many businesses, due to delays in jobs being completed, suppliers paying and deals closing. Suddenly, in comparison, our potential AU$280,000 loss over a month didn't seem so ridiculous. Their mouths didn't drop open in shock when I confessed what I was facing.

I'm not saying they belittled the risk – they were full of valuable advice – but they didn't overlay it with dramatics, theatrics or shrieks of, 'What on earth are you going to do now?' I get that, to an early-stage founder, a loss like this would leave them inconsolable. In *Daring & Disruptive*, I talked about the time I laid awake worrying about an AU$80 bill I couldn't pay. But it's incredible how your propensity for risk adapts in relation to your business experience.

When I'm having a shitty downturn, an experienced friend will say, 'Don't worry, I've just lost AU$7 million.' Of course, I'm not happy for their loss – I want EVERYONE to succeed together – but it does show the normalcy of the rollercoaster of business.

Now that I'm five years into *Collective Hub*, I hope I can offer perspective to other earlier-stage start-up founders, too. A few days ago, I received a phone call from a beautiful female founder working in the health space. Her second-in-command had just resigned and she was consumed with worry. "It's a disaster," she said. "What am going to do now?" I was able to tell her about the week I lost my entire sales team and how it turned into an incredibly positive step for the business, although it didn't feel that way at the time.

I always say that no matter what, we can always inspire people and people can always be inspired by us. We always sit generally somewhere in the middle as any individual at any stage in life. No matter how successful you might be, there are those that are so much more so. And there are those who have much to learn from you. I always find this really humbling. And I always find that it helps me keep perspective and also to keep grounded. It's the entire reason I'm writing this book, really. They say you're the average of the five people you spend the most time with. According to this concept, we're influenced by our core friends' attitude shifts, belief systems, self-esteem and decision-making abilities. This is never truer than when you're an entrepreneur in survival mode, attempting to keep a clear head as storm clouds circle above you.

I keep supporting and lifting those up that are not yet at the point of resilience, business, lessons or grit – or whatever it is that I am at, but I also know that I can ALWAYS, ALWAYS, ALWAYS keep learning from others.

It's also really important to keep perspective that business is just business. As much as we absolutely love it as founders – it's often our passion and our lifeblood – at the end of the day it's all just a game, really. What I've learnt more recently is to try not to get too attached to it, otherwise when you take a BIG hit, it's easy to go down with the ship and momentarily think your life is over.

At times like this, I'll chat to someone else and they'll share their story – which is generally equal to, or 10 times worse in magnitude to what I've just experienced – and yet they've lived to tell the tale. We get through things – always. In the moment it might feel like death – but we do get through it. There is no way I'd be able to remain as positive, optimistic, disruptive, and calm in a crisis without having incredible people around me, who can't necessarily share my load, but admit they've carried their own – and are still standing afterwards!

We asked...

SALLY OBERMEDER

After surviving cancer, Sally and sister Maha cofounded Swiish - an online destination offering luxe style for less.

HOW DO YOU BECOME YOUR OWN CHEERLEADER?

"One of the things that a lot of people will do when they want to make a big lifestyle change is ask everyone they know – from their friends and family to their colleagues – what they think. While it's great to get feedback from people who care about you, it's an even better idea to be your own encourager, and to trust your gut and go for what you think is best! Being your own cheerleader is the best thing you can do as a person – in particular, as an entrepreneur.

For me, when my sister Maha Koraiem and I wanted to start Swiish, a lot of people said to us that it was a ridiculous idea ('There are a million other blogs out there!'). While everyone is entitled to their opinion, and I appreciated their feedback, it was the gut instincts of Maha and I that made us persevere and create what we have now. We believed in our vision, and in sharing what we knew about how to live a truly fabulous life in a way that's affordable. So we became our own cheerleaders and that's all that really mattered.

A similar thing happened when Maha and I wanted to publish a smoothie recipe book. All the publishers said no, but we knew we had an excellent idea, so we decided to publish it ourselves. After all of the rejections from publishers and editors, and doubts from friends, family and industry colleagues, it hit number one on iTunes – and suddenly the publishers called us back. It went on to become the number one best-selling smoothie book in Australia, and top three non-fiction book of 2015.

When the first issue of Collective Hub *came out, we had only started Swiish about five months earlier. Since then, I can't even tell you how many pages I've torn out of the magazine and stuck to the inspiration board in my office. Whenever I read one of the issues or scroll through the Instagram feed, I instantly feel connected to the thousands of other readers and subscribers; I feel like we're all in it together.*

On a day-to-day basis, I get an idea and go for it. That sounds simple, and in a way it is. Don't get me wrong, the execution and the work that goes into it is hard! But the more you say, 'I'm going for it,' the easier it gets. Trust me. If something unexpected happens, or if something knocks you down, you have to pick yourself up and keep going.

When I was little and would have an idea, my mum used to say to me, 'I don't think you should do it, but if you think you should do it and you want to, then you should do it. You don't need my approval.' That's how I live, giving myself approval and being my own cheerleader. I always say to women, 'Go for it. You've got this.'

The power of *connection*

People come into your life when they're most needed. This applies whether they're romantic, platonic or professional relationships and interactions. Take my own dating history. When I needed high energy in the early stages of a business, I received it – in abundance – from my partner at the time. Before him, another partner helped me to heal my emotional wounds. My boyfriend now – the most kind, caring, selfless man on the planet – knows just what to say and has phenomenal experience in scaling and selling. He was a gift, exactly when I needed him and I'll never be able to thank him enough for his support and guidance.

You don't even have to search for these precious people. You just have to be open and let them find YOU. In times of crisis, it can be tempting to cut yourself off from the world and become an island. I've written in my previous books about my turbulent relationship with some of my family members and how we reconnected and fell in love again.

According to data from the General Social Survey, the number of Americans who say they have no close friends has roughly tripled in recent decades. When asked how many confidants they have, the most common answer among respondents was 'zero'. Another survey found that one in five female professionals don't have a mentor. That's a lot of entrepreneurs with nobody to confide in!

As a start-up founder, we can easily use work to avoid connecting ('Sorry, I'm working,' or 'Sorry, I'm sooo busy'). Of course, there are times when it's valuable to retreat and spend time in solitude to rest, recover and assess your future. But it's also important to surround yourself with positive people who won't sugarcoat your reality, but will support you through it.

Messages of support might come in unexpected forms, from unexpected places. In July, 2017, I was scrolling through Instagram when I saw a beautiful picture shared by the homewares start-up, The Design Twins – a big black and white photograph of one of the strongest faces I've ever seen. I was transfixed by her features. The image made me feel uplifted, inspired, strong, grounded and calm. I must have liked or commented on it.

The next morning, I woke up to a message from one of The Design Twin's co-founders, Crystal. "She is yours," it read. It was the most incredible gift at a time when I REALLY needed an emotional elevation. But, what happened next was even more amazing.

A few days later, Crystal personally delivered the beautiful piece to my office. As I wasn't there when she arrived, I shared the picture on Instagram and gave her a big shout-out. Here is what she replied via a direct message, that she's permitted me to share with you: "Three years ago I was an unemployed single mum in Tamworth, where I grew up. Then I met [my partner] Mitch and we ran away to Sydney. We had no money, so we started making concrete in our sink with a $10 bag of concrete. Within weeks we had people finding us on Instagram, and magazines and stylists wanting our products."

"Last month we opened a retail store in LA and next month in Byron. You inspire people like me who had no money, but big dreams. Thanks for supporting small businesses! Today we've had 10 people ring up wanting that same artwork. You're the best."

When I read that message I was sitting at home in my grey trackie dacks and Ugg boots, totally exhausted after a long day of meetings and feeling unusually depleted. I'm not big on accepting gifts from small brands, because I like to pay my way and support start-ups whose work I truly love. But it's also important not to turn away from generosity when it's offered with grace and kindness.

This wasn't about a physical painting, but the giver's intention. Just when I needed it, Crystal's words cut through my tiredness. They reminded me that, through *Collective Hub*, we ARE making a difference, in a way that can't always be measured by profit margins. What's more extraordinary, is it turns out Mitch once lived in my house in Bangalow, which I'd bought seven years earlier. When we transformed it into the Collective Retreat (more on that project later) they supplied pots for the fit-out. Now, if that's not serendipity and synchronicity at play…

I get literally hundreds of messages like Crystal's, every single day (although not everyone sends me wall art!). A day doesn't go by without my team and I speaking to, hearing from, or receiving a social message from someone who passionately proclaims they owe their career, happiness, relationship, health or new-found abundance to something they read in the mag that sparked an 'aha moment', which encouraged them to take action, move forward or make incredible changes.

It can be easy to forget you're doing something that really IS serving a purpose, especially when you get wrapped up in problem-solving all day long. The night I hung the print from The Design Twins in my living room, I wrote in my journal, "Bloody hell. What a privilege!!! No money worries in the world could take away the impact that *Collective Hub* is having. And so…

I will keep fighting to see another day"

Be grateful,
give back,
the world
wants to
support
YOU

The gift of praise

Sometimes you need to put distance between yourself and 'normal' life to find perspective. This was brought home to me when I flew to San Francisco and attended the Dreamforce conference in 2017, a 'global gathering for trailblazers', where the incredible speakers included Will.I.Am, Michelle Obama, Marc Benioff and Ashton Kutcher.

It was a last minute trip, supported by Air New Zealand, and so I didn't have much time to organise my itinerary. On the way there – literally while waiting at the departure gate – I fired off a bunch of emails to department heads at Facebook, Instagram, Airbnb and Google asking if I could come by their headquarters for a meeting – and every one of them said yes.

It seemed unbelievable for our Aussie-grown brand. Each of my (unsolicited!) emails was met with a reply from someone I'd never met or spoken to, saying how much they LOVED our magazine and would be thrilled to meet us.

A few days later, I found myself at Facebook HQ having an intimate behind-the-scenes tour, which included riding a bike around Building 20 where the inspirational Mark and Sheryl both reside. I also discovered that one of Facebook's senior staff members has been spreading our magazine throughout the company's talented global team since issue one. Who knew we had a secret support network in the Valley?

On another day, I spent an unforgettable morning at Airbnb HQ, where I was moved to tears by a huge diagram across one wall, showing their disaster response efforts. Today, as part of their Open Homes initiative, more than 3500 homes have been opened – free of charge – to people in need of shelter.

As I flew back to Sydney, I felt inspired, uplifted and rejuvenated. It would have been very easy for me to cancel that trip, which took place at a time when

Collective Hub's future was still very unclear. I could have stayed chained to my desk, but instead I chose to step outside my comfort zone, consciously and purposefully, to seek outside influences – and it paid off in every way.

Not only did it give me an opportunity to rest (we stayed at the amazing Farmhouse Inn in Sonoma County between tech meetings), but I had the big realisation that, when I had a bigger team, I was sometimes at arm's length (and quite frankly had levels of gatekeepers) from just how sticky and alive the *Collective Hub* brand had become. Connecting to people outside your organisation can be a wake-up call that everything is WAY better than you gave it credit for. From a financial viewpoint, I also made invaluable connections which later paid off generously. These BIG meetings took me away from some of the day-to-day minutiae I had been forced to do – jumping on calls to kids at media agencies trying to buy my soul for AU$3000 a pop... This trip enabled me to have very big, very real-world changing, deep conversations with some of the biggest thinkers and game changers on the planet. Sometimes it's just this external injection that enables you to go back in fighting and believing in your cause all over again.

I have endless examples of times when a beautiful friendship, connection or collaboration has lifted me higher. In my morale-boosting toolkit I store many memorable moments: shooting beautiful videos with bestselling author Danielle LaPorte; visiting Necker Island to pitch to Sir Richard Branson; the many incredible entrepreneurs, thought-leaders and trend-setters who contributed content to our 50th anniversary issue and were just as excited as us when the magazine hit the shelves.

I have written in my previous books about the support crew that can help a start-up to function – CFOs, accountants, lawyers, contributors and freelancers. But there is also a lot to be said for 'non-hireables' – people who CHOOSE to support you, rather than being paid to. These are your army. Your evangelists. The truth is, it's easy to be brought down by naysayers.

And some people LOVE drama and, at the first hint of trouble, will be quick to tell you it's irreversible. That's why I value, honour and commit time and energy to the people in my life who are calm, uplifting and empowering, even in times of adversity.

This isn't about surrounding yourself with 'yes' people (a terrible business strategy!). The best confidants don't always say that you're right, but even manage to say you're wrong with grace, respect and gentleness. I ALWAYS make sure I thank these people for coming into my world, whether our connection consists of one social media message or a friendship that has lasted a decade.

This is an email I sent to an incredible friend after our drastic scale-down period, when he took the time to talk me through the steps, despite being incredibly busy with his own global platform.

"Your words really helped me so so much," I wrote. "Just knowing that someone else had been through something similar to what I was experiencing in the moment gave it some perspective… While we are a long way from being out of the woods, I certainly feel like I have the resilience and the tenacity to stick in there and fight and do what I need to do to propel us forward.

"The future looks a lot brighter… and I wanted to say THANK YOU. Because it was your two emails and your kindness at EXACTLY the right moment that is entirely the reason I now feel strong enough to tackle this next phase. Biggest love to you, my incredible, amazing, kind, big-hearted friend."

"THE BEST BUSINESS ADVICE I EVER RECEIVED…"

IN THE LEAD-UP TO OUR 2017 KICK. START. SMART. EVENT, WE ASKED SPEAKERS TO SHARE THE GREATEST WORDS OF ADVICE THEY'D RECEIVED

MATT JONES

CO-FOUNDER AND DIRECTOR OF FOUR PILLARS GIN

"Every mistake hurts, and I take every mistake stupidly seriously and then, having learnt the lesson, I try to let it go. I'm just lucky that most of the big mistakes and failures in my career have led me to where I am today, which is a pretty fortunate place to be. There's no point dwelling on them. You just need to learn the crap out of them."

STUART GREGOR

CO-FOUNDER AND DIRECTOR FOUR PILLARS GIN

"Invest your hard-earned money in the things you know more about than most other people."

ANDRIANES PINANTOAN

HEAD OF GROWTH AT CANVA

"Don't compare your behind-the-scenes to other people's highlights. Highlights are all we see in articles. What we don't see — because people don't publicise it — are all the struggles behind the scenes."

JAYE EDWARDS

FOUNDER OF EDWARDS AND CO.

"Success doesn't come easy. I wish I knew of the sleepless nights, the stress, the fights, and everything in between that comes from building an expanding business. But you know what? It's worth it!"

VICTORIA BEATTIE

CO-FOUNDER AND DIRECTOR OF THE BEACH PEOPLE

"It's going to be more amazing than you think, it's going to take more out of you than you think, it's going to be tougher than you think, and it's going to be more magical than you think. Oh, the highs and lows of entrepreneurial life."

EMMA HENDERSON

CO-FOUNDER AND DIRECTOR OF THE BEACH PEOPLE

"Live the life you want to live now... don't wait or say 'Once this or that happens, I will be this kinda person.' Be the person and live the kinda life you want today."

HAYDEN COX

FOUNDER OF HAYDENSHAPES

"Create something that is measurably better. In not just one way, but at least three. That's advice given to me by Jim Jannard, creator of Oakley, when I interviewed him for my book, New Wave Vision.

"My first lesson in starting a business is that you should always be two steps ahead, not behind. I don't think I really knew how much work, time, blood, sweat and tears would be required in making my brand what it is today, but I wouldn't change anything. This year, it turns 20."

JODIE FOX

CO-FOUNDER OF SHOES OF PREY

"Do everything before you're ready and fail fast — these are two mantras you'll hear me repeat time and time again. The former is something that I've had to learn to do and has become my business mantra. The latter is advice I was given by one of my co-founders, Mike Knapp, when we were starting Shoes of Prey. I still find both statements invaluable to this day. They are examples of the mindset that has been so important to our success."

Chapter Seven

Searching for
salvation

CHAPTER SEVEN

Searching for ~~salvation~~

In year one of *Collective Hub*, when our mission was really only just getting started, someone offered me AU$1 million for 10 per cent of the company. Less than 12 months after launching, they gave us a AU$10 million valuation. It was a very serious offer, which came from a very serious investor who could have brought added value to the business, both financially and professionally. But I turned her down.

Was I crazy? I stand by my choices – always. As I wrote in my book *Money & Mindfulness*, most entrepreneurs are fiercely independent, with a stubborn streak and don't really like to answer to others. Isn't this why we decided to go it alone, pursue our passions and chase a career without compromise in the first place?

In the early stages of the magazine, I just didn't want anyone else slowing me down. As my amazing team will tell you (or warn you), I move at an extremely relentless, fast pace when it comes to making, changing and switching decisions, forever reacting and reassessing so that our brand evolves, improves and keeps one step ahead of other market leaders.

How would I move at this speed if I had multiple stakeholders to check in with and multiple opinions to consider? I've spoken to other magazine editors and publishers who have to wait for approval from five different people in five different countries to change the colour of a single full stop on a masthead.

I still stand by this decision, firmly and boldly. If I had accepted that investment in year one, I know *Collective Hub* would be a very different entity today. And I wouldn't be able to stand here, hand on heart, and say that I'd followed my dream without compromise.

However, there is a time and a place for everything. On an unforgettable Monday in mid-December, 2016, I walked into the office, clear as anything, and said, "Let's build to sell." In more than 15 years since starting my first business, I had never uttered these words. Not once. But suddenly, as everything was imploding around me, there came many realisations and wonderful learnings. It became hugely apparent that, while our vision was unwavering, on my own I didn't have the resources to make *Collective Hub* everything it needed to be – and everything that our community deserved.

What were we really building towards? What was our end game? What were we aiming for? To reinvigorate me and my executive team, I needed to create a goal post – something to aim for. Even if it would turn out to be a false one, should we re-fall in love with the business, it became acutely apparent that we needed to have a collective end game. It was time we looked for investment, which could either mean I sold a small stake in the company or the entire brand – and walked away completely. (Okay, who am I kidding – if that was to happen I would always remain the face of the company, or involved in some way... but it was time to explore all options)

So began the biggest challenge, and steepest learning curve, that I've ever faced in my entrepreneurial career – to take my baby out to the market. I've always said I'm not anti-investor – far from it, and in a different iteration of a new business I may well go after investors from the get-go, rather than bear the financial burden day in, day out myself. But, if and when I choose to part with a portion of my brand's equity, I always promise to do it at my own pace, in my own way, on my own terms, at the right time for my company. Well, it felt like the time was now.

And so, the following week, my consultant and I arranged a meeting with a mergers and acquisitions company who would start the process of looking for buyers. Because I have ALWAYS promised to be honest with our community, I announced our decision to seek investors in my Founder's Letter in our 50th anniversary issue: "This lil' country kid has taken it as far as she can alone. Who knows what will happen next, but the big vision is set and so I have no doubt it will be exciting."

It was time to spread my wings – or at least stretch them out a little

We asked...

MANDI GUNSBERGER

Mandi Gunsberger, founder of *Babyology*, which the mother-of-three built from scratch and sold in 2017 to Kinderling Kids Radio for an undisclosed (but life-changing!) sum.

HOW DID IT FEEL TO SELL YOUR CREATION?

"Wow, a business exit can be more traumatic, complicated and much harder work than I ever thought possible. It can take a lot longer than planned and deadlines that are set by both parties drag out over many months. First, I want to make it clear this is only my experience. Every business and acquisition is different and I can only tell you what I did, and how I felt during it. With that in mind, here are some tips that have come from my recent business acquisition process.

Choose an adviser who you really, really like, to run the process with you. You are trusting this person with your asset; your baby you have worked hard on for many years. You want it in good hands! You will most likely speak to your adviser at least once a day for the duration of the process, which can be many months. They are there to explain what is happening, all the steps, the finances, legals and deal structure. Do not only choose an adviser based on the retainer or commission structure, it also needs to be someone who is well-liked in your industry and who potential buyers want to work with and trust.

Be prepared to do many pitches. Know that potential buyers will want to know EVERYTHING about your business. They need to be excited about the opportunity it holds, so come up with a pitch that captures all it has to offer and what the future can hold. Craft a story around how the business started, how it has grown and all the achievements along the way and back this up with compelling stats and financials. Paint a positive picture into the future, too, to give them reassurance the business is facing forward. Well presented financials can paint this picture nicely and create excitement.

Not all exits come when you are ready or planning to sell the business. We were only looking for investment when we began to get offers to acquire Babyology. I have always found it useful to run the business with the thought that, if I were approached today by a potential buyer, would the financials be up to date and ready for someone to dig into the guts of the business? If you are ready to exit, target a list of potential bidders. To get a good price you need to show a history of steady growth and also recurring revenue from customers ideally locked into the company for a certain period of time.

How would the business run without you involved? Spend some time thinking about this possibility. Allow staff to be trained and have the authority they need to succeed and make decisions. I deliberately scaled back my involvement in some areas, delegated small big decisions, was less available for clients and let the sales team close larger deals, and came and went from the office more often. You want to ensure the business continues to thrive after you've left.

We moved the business into a permanent headquarters. Before, I worked from a home office with 20 remote staff. This was a conscious, strategic decision. It's much easier to review a business that has regular office expenses and a local team, than a remote business run from home as many of the costs will be unknown. This could take time to work through, and personally took us a few years to transform the business from a home business where I had many roles, to a HQ where I had staff for all the various areas of the business.

Be impeccable with organisation as you look to hand over the reins. You need to have formal, efficient processes documented. From the beginning of my business we created a cloud-based wiki, which started off simply and grew into a mammoth document of over 350 pages. This was the bible on all things relating to the business. Everything from org charts to staff birthdays, new-starter checklists, monthly targets and details of all software systems. This made the handover to the buyer so much easier and allowed me to step out of the business straight away – and head to Japan with my family for a six-week holiday!

I live, giving myself approval and being my own cheerleader. I always say to women, 'Go for it. You've got this.'"

Now or never

When is the right time to sell? It's a question that many entrepreneurs grapple with and also disagree about. Hit Google and you'll find a confusing mash-up of conflicting advice pedalled by experts.

Arianna Huffington and her co-founders sold *The Huffington Post* to AOL six years after it was founded for a cool US$315 million. Michael Arrington sold TechCrunch, also to AOL, for a reported US$30 million five years after launch. There are some that wait longer and some who take the step sooner. YouTube had been around for less than two years when Google bought it in 2006, and Skype wasn't much older when eBay bought it in 2005.

The same range of advice applies when it comes to investment – when to ask for it, and when to accept it. You can look for investors pre-revenue, before you've even sold a single product, or wait until you have a customer base to prove that your company is valuable.

For issue 52 of *Collective Hub*, we interviewed Melanie Perkins, co-founder of design platform Canva which, in 2017, became Australia's newest unicorn after a funding round put their valuation above US$1 billion. Melanie, who launched her first start-up at university, was only 30 years old at the time, and the start-up was only five years old. "We feel like we're a baby unicorn right now," she told us. "We have so much room to grow and expand. We've only done one per cent of what we believe is possible."

When it comes to when and how to get investment, I don't think there's a one-size-fits-all approach. With Canva, Melanie won over infamous Silicon Valley venture capitalist Bill Tai by learning how to kitesurf. "I had a brief encounter with Bill at a Perth conference in 2010," she recalled. "I discovered

Bill was part of a kitesurfing and entrepreneurship conference in Hawaii. So, [my partner] Cliff and I decided to learn how to kitesurf so we could be a part of it. Fun fact – that network made up a lot of the initial investment in Canva."

You can read every how-to article on bagging investment but, at its core, you have to trust your gut, stick to your ethos and think about what's best for yourself and also your community. I would never tell ANYONE when it's time to seek funding. All I can share is the reasons behind my personal decision and the signs to look out for.

For me, it was a mixture of personal, emotional and professional triggers. I felt a constant, aching weariness. To put this in perspective – compared to the average Joe I was still 100,000,000 per cent happier, more buoyant and driven than anyone around me. But I do remember one weekday morning, after a particularly fierce stretch of events across the country and a journey back from Italy, waking up at 3.30pm – crazy! I had the worst dreams and woke up feeling beyond horrid, with 26 missed calls from my partner and employees frantic with worry about me. Jetlag had hit, and it had hit hard.

I also had an odd sense that life was moving on without me. I loved my current team who were so incredibly passionate about the brand and our future. But none of them had been with me more than a year (apart from my Contributing Editor who worked remotely). Of my core team, two had recently left to have babies and two more were blooming bumps. Times were changing, and it felt like a natural time for a new iteration for everyone.

I had also recently returned from three weeks spent in Italy which, as well as a much-needed holiday, had doubled as a business experiment. I wanted to test two things while I was in Europe. 1) Is *Collective Hub* a sustainable business? And 2) Is it sustainable without me? The first question got a yes, although we were still only just breaking even at this time. The second part was a resounding no – not without me, not as it stood in its current form. In the six weeks prior to Italy, not a day went by that we weren't doing one to four deals, yet for the time I was away only two deals were done in total – one for AU$25,000 and one for AU$4,000 which put us behind again. At this point, my sales team was very new and still finding their feet. But it did bring home the realisation that I was far too pivotal to the brand's success – which isn't the way to create a sustainable company or a positive legacy that will be able to live on beyond you.

It's an important message: when you think something is your baby and you're so attached, you have to take the time and space to lift beyond that. Am I overattached to this thing I love more than anything on the planet? And, is it overattached to me, too?

PREPPING TO IMPRESS

It's a very odd and somewhat liberating feeling prepar ng your brand for possible investment or exit. The first step was a meeting with a boutique M&A advisory firm who had a LOT of experience in media brand sales and acquisitions. In the lead-up to the meeting I reached out to a few trusted confidants who had experience in selling and buying businesses. This is some of the amazing advice I got from them:

IT'S IMPORTANT TO NEVER APPEAR DESPERATE FOR A SALE
The top line is: biz is good, we've turned the corner, brand equity is second to none and there are lots of opportunities to monetise.

TRY TO DEMONSTRATE THE BRAND EQUITY
Include total followers – but it's much deeper than that. Is there a way that you can demonstrate everything the brand encompasses, that's not directly linked to you?

WHY ARE YOU DIFFERENT? How are you better than the other media guys? You almost want them to put you in a different category.

YOU HAVE A PRETTY UNIQUE YOUNG FEMALE FOLLOWING
That's a crazy part of your brand. They trust you, they love you, they will follow anything you do. This is powerful!

IS THERE CHEMISTRY BETWEEN YOU AND POTENTIAL INVESTORS? Most importantly, do you like them? Do you trust them?

JUST ENJOY IT!
This is a big step! So enjoy it. Yes, even on the toughest days.

@LISAMESSENGER

To my surprise, I did find the process of preparing for the meeting with the agency enjoyable – although time-consuming! It was a little like when I prepared my entry for the first round of Telstra Business Women's Awards back in 2007, where I had to gather every bit of information about me to date – it was a great exercise in getting all my ducks in a row! In fact, it's an exercise I would highly recommend as a continuous ritual throughout your business life. So that when you need it most, you have a presentation ready to go.

Venture capitalist Jamie Pride, author of the book *Unicorn Tears: Why start-ups fail and how to avoid it*, has more than 20 years' experience building and investing in companies. He says there is a formula to raising capital, which he calls the 5 Ps of funding fitness:

- PERSONA (choosing the right investor)
- PROOF (what traction have you had to date)
- PREP (getting your business ready to raise)
- PROCESS (managing a structured process for capital raising)
- PITCH (making your investment value proposition)

I won't sugarcoat it – preparing to pitch for investment is a testing and, at times, intimidating process, but also incredibly rewarding. Along with my CFO and consultant, we spent a few weeks going backwards and forwards gathering the relevant materials from the past five years, preparing an overview of *Collective Hub*. Why I set up the brand, what we've achieved, what I'd like to see it become and why I'd reached the decision that an exit is a viable option. It sounded strange and impersonal to bullet-point our journey, but it had to be done for clarity.

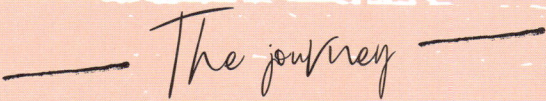

— The journey —

X The business was travelling very well for the first few years of its life.

X At the start of the last financial year, the business increased investment in the management and sales team; this didn't work out, with revenue increase not offsetting the additional costs.

X Since then, we've dialled back to a simpler business model and right now are breaking even.

X The real growth potential lies in developing digital events and training products. Our community loves our Masterclass product – both for 'hard skills' and for empowerment. There's potential for huge growth in this market.

X With a modest amount of investment we could drive scale in the Masterclass business and shore up the sales team to ensure break even or better results.

X It's likely that a larger publisher will have more success in driving revenue for the media side of the business (more briefs, larger team).

I also made it clear that I was fully committed to the brand going forward and, if it did get a new owner, that I'd still love to be involved as a CEO, creative director, brand ambassador, business consultant or some combination of these.

There are many ways of selling all or some of a company (which you'll read about in the section below). For us, potential investors included banks, financial investors, strategic investors and brokerage. A lot of independent media brands are eventually bought out by the big guns – think *Kidspot* (bought by News Corp), *Pedestrian* (which sold a large stake to Nine Entertainment), *Junkee* (bought by oOh! Media Limited), and housed within their portfolio – not an idea I was initially keen on).

I even reached out to Sir Richard Branson and Chuck Townsend. There was also another, less conventional option. The M&A agency has always done straight media-to-media investments or exits. When I said, "I want to do a strategic deal with an Airbnb, Uber or Facebook," they were confused. "But, we've never heard of that." To me, it felt like the perfect solution. Especially since it hadn't been heard of by a traditional agency. I've never done things according to the status quo… why start now?

Since launch, I was determined that *Collective Hub* would be a global brand. Rather than combining with an Australia media biz, someone like an Airbnb, Uber or WeWork – companies we already had excellent, deep, longer term relationships with – would give us hugely exciting opportunities to grow, scale and have a bigger global footprint instantly.

Here's a thought… Uber launched in Australia around the same time as *Collective Hub* started. We have had a great relationship with David Rohrsheim, general manager of Uber Australia and New Zealand, since launch. Back in the day they only had around 50 drivers. For the first year or so there was a copy of *Collective Hub* in the back of every Uber – a brilliant example of a cross-promotional relationship.

Fast-forward five years and, in a recent meeting with David, he mentioned they now have 70,000-odd drivers in Australia alone. As soon as he told me that, I identified two potential markets for us within the Uber camp. First, MANY of those drivers (I catch an Uber nearly every day and chat to every single one) are budding entrepreneurs, with fledgling start-ups or side-hustles they juggle on top of driving. They all NEED inspiration and education, and *Collective Hub* is the perfect base product to provide this. Sure, we don't have the scale that they have, but we've sure as hell built a scalable product that they could tap into. And then there is the Uber customer. Although it might not be feasible to physically put a print magazine in the back of 70,000 or so cars, imagine if we could digitise this content and interlink it with the Uber app? Not only would you book your car, but straight away you would get access to some of the most incredible digital content to inspire you.

This is just one quick brain-dump for one possible collaboration. When we were thinking of possible investors, I let my imagination run wild. I also did a LOT of research which backed up my prediction – the world's most disruptive companies WERE interested in investment in, or buying out, brands in different industries that were adjacent to their core strategies.

Take Airbnb as an example. Their acquisitions do include smaller players in the travel market (Vamo, GetspotOn and Crashpadder). They acquired a 100 per cent stake in Accomable Limited – a service to help people with mobility difficulties find accessible properties.

However, their deals also include left-field buyouts that are far more unexpected. Tilt – a funding platform for brands and businesses to collect, fundraise, or pool money. Lapka, a Russian industrial design firm which created smartphone-assisted breathalysers. They also acquired the majority of the team from Changecoin, a bitcoin-based micro-payments service company.

How could *Collective Hub* combine powerfully with another disruptor? Why limit ourselves to media organisations when there are so many incredible brands in so many incredible industries kicking arse and sharing our rebellious ethos?

After my recent trip to San Francisco, Airbnb seemed like a prime place to begin. While touring the rental platform's amazing headquarters in San Francisco, I'd connected with a bunch of people in their senior management team. Amazingly, one of the brand's co-founders, Joe Gebbia, was about to fly to Australia to launch their Experiences platform in Melbourne (*Collective Hub* was also due to shoot him for an exclusive article, and he and I ended up making a number of pieces-to-camera together). I arranged a meeting with their head of alternative marketing channels, which took place the week after our photoshoot.

It felt so serendipitous – a message from the universe! So began a period of intense strategising and researching to ensure that we were confident and totally pitch-perfect. When I'm on stage I love nothing more than spontaneously riffing, but even I know there's a time and a place for doing intricate preparation.

In the slideshow we prepared, we split our company overview into clear, kick-arse sections, which began with an executive summary...

EXECUTIVE SUMMARY

EXCEPTIONAL BRAND AWARENESS AND LOYALTY
- The *Collective Hub* brand has a loyal and passionate following.
- The brand has permission to be audacious, innovative and disruptive.

PROVEN OFFERING TO A VALUABLE AUDIENCE
- Commercial partners acknowledge that impact and engagement go far beyond typical media metrics.
- Our high engagement levels open up to new opportunities.

EXPERIENCED AND PASSIONATE TEAM
- Lisa Messenger is an authority for entrepreneurs.
- Real talent in content and sales...
- ... with capacity for so much more.
- Flexible, responsive culture.

STRONG GROWTH POTENTIAL
- Room for growth within existing business lines.
- Many dimensions for growth remain to be seized, but resource constraints limit the vision.

CLEAR STRATEGY

- ✗ Clear strategy for growth with care.
- ✗ Each segment has clear proven business model and growth potential.
- ✗ That said, many new areas remain to be explored.
- ✗ The path forward will vary according to the strategic partner.

RARE OPPORTUNITY

- ✗ To tap into a much-loved multimedia movement with exponential opportunity for growth.
- ✗ To extend your market and reach by tapping into our existing assets to champion the power of individual voices, shared ideas and experiences.
- ✗ To use the influence of Lisa Messenger and our passionate community to drive into new territory; supporting the start-up community, igniting human potential, and inspiring entrepreneurial thinking globally.

I would love to share EVERY detail of every meeting we held with potential investors (#openbook), but I have to protect the confidentiality of the people we met and spoke to. Let's just say, every meeting was incredibly different. Some felt like a perfect fit and others less so. When it comes to making deals worth tens of millions (or deals worth $1000), the outcome is based on so many things – timing, priorities, budget, how much the person on the other end knows about you. And, whether they're the right person to be speaking to at all!

After one meeting, my consultant turned to me and said, "I think I need to lay in a dark room for a while." It was an exhilarating process, but also incredibly complex and energy consuming. I certainly wasn't going to go out with a bang, right?

One of the best pieces of advice I can offer ANY entrepreneur – even if right now you think you'll never sell – is to network and be a connector, no matter what stage you're at in business. I CANNOT begin to tell you how easy arranging these meetings was (and to be honest, how fun it was) because I had networked so enthusiastically over the past 15.5 years in the start-up world.

Every meeting I tried to organise to chat about various potential investment channels received a resounding yes. Not one person didn't want to meet with me. Suddenly it became a fun game of Tetris. I LOVE nothing more than lots of moving parts and options. As an entrepreneur, you have GOT to have options. You never want to be in a position where your back is up against the wall and you don't have choice. So this became my game. And this gave me a renewed sense of hunger across every aspect of the business.

I loved it so much that when none of the meetings turned into the right offer (some figures were too low, some said it was the wrong time, some had other priorities, some were just not going to take care of my baby as it deserved…) I was able to see the invaluable lessons I got from the process.

Every meeting was an education – about my brand, about the industry, about collaboration, cooperation and the possibilities in front of me. I learnt a lot. About investment. About human nature. I saw the best and I saw the worst in people. One of the greatest realisations is that however big and loved your brand is, you are in it alone at the end of the day. And you just have to keep believing in yourself.

Out of the conversation with Airbnb I learnt a lot more about their own in-house magazine, and the potential ways we could work together in the future. From connecting with Facebook, I got on the radar of their new women's network, and began discussing becoming an adviser for them.

I had to learn when to quit in terms of too much attachment to *Collective Hub*, which at the time was like fitting a square peg into a round hole in its current format with Airbnb's current strategies and vision.

I also learnt a lot about my limits and the compromises I WASN'T prepared to make, just to get money. After a meeting with a big Australian media company, who wooed us with talk of a podcast, television show and me running a couple of their other women's assets, I received an apologetic email (not even a phone call) saying it, "isn't the right time for us". However, if we could "adjust the price", they could "fit us into their brand somewhere".

It's heartbreaking to hear a brand you've put your heart and soul into spoken about as if it's an inconvenience. I've built *Collective Hub* on a promise that, to succeed, you have to be big and bold, shooting for the stars and shouting your hopes from the rooftops. No amount of money could make me bury my brand in something else. I owed it to our community and everyone who had ever supported us to stay true to our mission and be loud, proud and unapologetically 'us' until the end – whatever that end might be.

Maybe I could have kept chasing the investment thread. Maybe I could have gone back and convinced people. But I needed to get back to our immediate monetary partnerships and focus on keeping us going. It could have taken me another six months to talk to the person at Airbnb, for example, to try and do a deal. But with every investment meeting I began to reassess my options.

Never be driven by desperation. That's what I realised was so important. Desperate is never a good headspace to be in, because you make silly decisions and knee-jerk reactions rather than informed decisions.

I discovered that searching for investment had an amazing side effect – it made me crystal-clear about my intentions. I came into this iteration of my journey saying, "While I might own this brand 100 per cent financially, I don't OWN it. Our community owns it." And I certainly owed it to all of you to do what would be best for it at this stage.

Many of you will know, as it has been well documented in my own books and writing, as well as by the greater media, that *Collective Hub* has NEVER been about a print magazine – it has been about igniting human potential.

This was now more apparent than ever. But it was becoming increasingly clear that I couldn't elevate our community in the way it deserved when I was bogged down with the exhausting task of simple survival.

Imagine what we could be if we were free from our baggage?

So, after weeks of intense meetings that matched the G-force of any rollercoaster, I went away to Byron Bay for four weeks to reassess my options (while still working remotely). That's when I came up with the plan for *Collective Hub* 2.0 – a new iteration for the brand, and for myself. As I pondered this thought – long and HARD – a realisation began to drop into my mind. A new direction started to form in my head: a new way forward which could set us free to soar.

Ready? Read on...

5 Lessons I learnt (failing) to get investment

1. **A YEAR MAKES A DIFFERENCE** I don't regret – not one little bit – turning down the investment offer in year one. I would have made the same decision up until year three. But, in retrospect, I think I should have started looking for investment in year four of my business, rather than waiting for our fifth birthday. By this stage, the media industry was really beginning to look dismal. It's testament to the power of our brand that I even got meetings when I was proposing a media sale with a print magazine at its core in this market.

2. **POWER UP YOUR PEOPLE** I've always cultivated a transparent company culture, so I was very honest with my (scaled down) team about my decision. This meant I was able to engage their skills in the process. My art director laid out our pitch deck, my partnership person gathered statistics, my digital editor subbed the deck and my CFO came in on her day off (with kids in tow) to rehearse our spiel. I couldn't have done it without them – and I wouldn't have wanted to. And my print editor is editing this book in real time – so she knows everything. There is beauty in all of this.

3. **DON'T MAKE YOUR POOL TOO SMALL** When we started searching for investors, I declared I would never approach a big media corporate. It seemed to go against everything I've said about flouting the system, breaking the rules and going against the status quo. But I learnt more from these meetings than possibly any others – even if it was only what I DIDN'T want. I'd hate to look back now and think, 'What if I missed out on an opportunity?' At least I can honestly say I tried every avenue, even when my heart wasn't 100 per cent in it.

4. WHAT DOES EVERYONE SAY? It's not always easy to accept feedback but, sometimes, when you hear the same message over and over you have to stop and listen. In every meeting I heard, 'We love *Collective Hub* and we think it has HUGE potential'. But...? 'The print magazine seems like too big a risk, financially.' This feedback, although hard for my ego, became key to our future – and my biggest, boldest plan yet! There was absolute gold in this. A brand that was loved by millions. But that no one would invest in at this time.

5. BE UNAFRAID TO LOSE IT ALL THIS has been my biggest lesson so far, and one that has taken so long to get to. I had to go through every iteration, every up and down, every trial and tribulation mentioned so far in this book to know that I'd given it EVERYTHING. Only then could I be okay with potentially walking away from everything we'd built to date. As I'll explain in the next chapter (the REALLY juicy twist in the story!), don't be attached to outcome. Surrender. As I stepped into a new reality of 'let it burn / break it all', I knew that my purpose was stronger than ever. It was the delivery mechanism – a print magazine – that had never really mattered.

The ins and outs of investment

A t one of *Collective Hub*'s Kick. Start. Smart. events, Mark McDonald, the technology entrepreneur who co-founded Appster when he was just 19 years old broke down how and where to get funding. Our community loved Mark's presentation so much, here are some of the highlights.

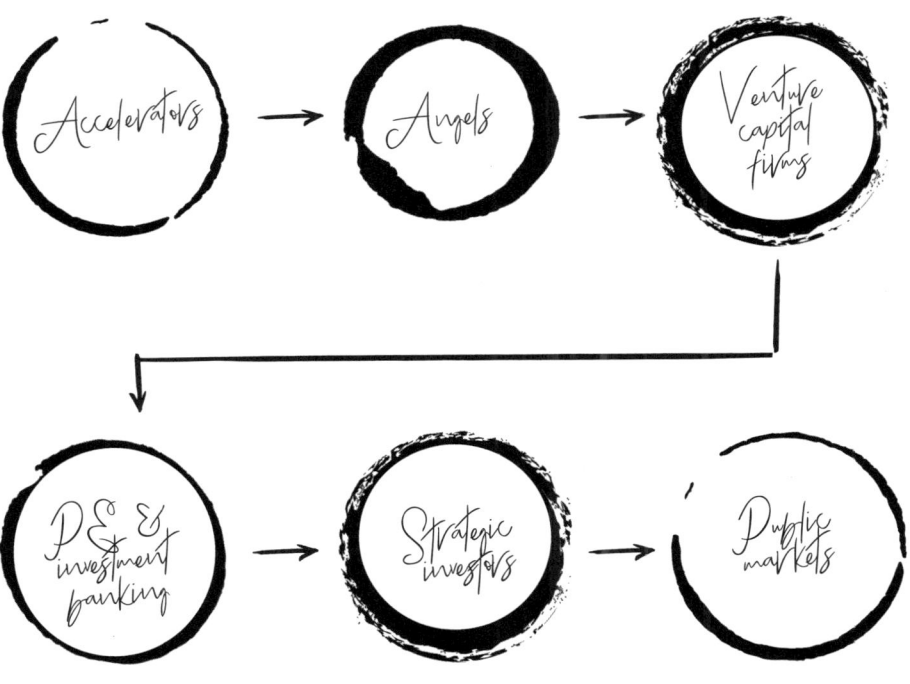

IMAGE @Appster

EQUITY FUNDING:
THE OPTIONS

How to choose an accelerator

✗ FOUNDERS
Do the partners, founders, or whatever they call them, have
a track record of running their own successful start-ups?

✗ MENTORS
Request a list of the mentors you will have access to. Make sure
they have experience in your industry.

✗ NETWORK
Do they offer a substantial network of alumni and mentors that can
help start-ups get in touch with potential customers, distribution channels etc?

✗ INVESTMENT
Find data on their alumni, how much they raised and compare.
Crunchbase or Seed-DB can be valuable tools for this.

How to find an angel investor

✗ ANGEL INVESTORS ARE basically rich individuals who invest in
start-ups. An ideal angel investor is an ex-entrepreneur with a successful
exit, preferably in your industry.

✗ ASIDE FROM MONEY, THEY BRING expertise, credibility and contacts.

X You can find them in a local angel association, on networking events, or using an angel list search.

X AngelList is an online angel investor / start-up community that allows angels to invest in featured start-ups directly, or by using syndicated investments.

How to secure venture capital

X VENTURE CAPITAL FIRMS ARE managed funds that invest in companies in multiple stages.

X THE PARTNERS ARE either professional VCs or, in a better case, ex-entrepreneurs. Like angels, they provide advice, network and expertise, but the amount of capital they provide is much more substantial.

X HOWEVER, UNLIKE ANGELS, they have their own investors, who are their clients, and thus they are pressured to show results fast.

X MANY PARTNERS AT VC FIRMS ARE FORMER ENTREPRENEURS themselves or have worked with enough entrepreneurs to know how to predict success and failure.

X WHILE VCS BRING IMMEDIATE CREDIBILITY to a company, they are under extreme pressure to maximise short-term value so that they can exit and realise their return.

X YOU CAN FIND a decent list of VC firms on mattermark.com/app/ Benchmarking. For more information visit AppsterHQ.com

Chapter Eight

When the industry
is crumbling

CHAPTER EIGHT

When the industry is ~~crumbling~~

A few days after I had the phone call from my M&A agency saying they were no longer exploring options for sale or investment, I received an email from the former chairman of a huge global media company, which helped me to understand what we were up against. For a long time, the most influential person in publishing on the planet, this person – who I can't name for obvious reasons – had always been incredibly kind to me.

In a casual way, he'd become an adviser and definitely a friend. In the past year, he'd chosen to step back (although, not down!) from the company he'd been part of for multiple decades. When *Collective Hub* was looking for investment, I'd reached out to see if he thought I should contact them – and his answer amazed me.

"There's no more M&A group here," he wrote. "Acquisitions seem to be happening but they are all small digital/software plays… and for the most part, it's divestiture and downsizing." In his next sentence, he revealed the ballpark number the company had lost in revenue the past two consecutive years – and it had eight figures!

This is a media company that, to the outside world, is the best of the best; scaling, monopolising and growing. Yet, even they were struggling in an industry that was changing and, some would say, crumbling. Their portfolio of print magazine runs into the hundreds, the cover stars they have access to is breathtaking and their fashion shoots must cost a fortune. But behind the curtain is it a different story?

It's a strange feeling to learn the company seen as being at the peak of your industry is actually struggling as much as you are – should you feel comforted or terrified?

Over the past five years I'd trained myself to rise above the closures and growing despair in the media industry. With every announcement I've had deep sympathy for everyone involved but I didn't obsess about having the same fate as them. Instead, I've used it to fuel my own 'let's not sit on our laurels' attitude. Rather than burying my head in the sand, I read every article that comes through about a closure – and I forward it onto my team to read, too.

It seems every industry faces questions about its future, as there's constant debate over which product will die out, and which people-manned roles will be replaced by artificial intelligence. Hell, throughout my time writing and consulting I've been asked by practically every kind of corporate across multiple industries and geographic locations about how they can stay relevant, disrupt and stay ahead of the curve.

All doom and gloom? It could be, if you were a glass-half-empty person. But I've always had a limitless 'you can just refill it' attitude. I knew exactly what I was getting into when I launched *Collective Hub*, despite the fact I had zero experience in the print magazine market. I knew – because people were lining up to tell me – that print sales were struggling and industry experts believed it was unsolvable.

I've (stubbornly!) refused to listen to the 'print is dead' naysayers. In fact, they only lit a fire underneath my mission. I've always believed that, with the right content – focusing on positive inspiration rather than celebrity gossip and bitchy commentary – there was still an important market for print magazines, which are both uplifting in their words and beautiful in their designs. And I'd proved it, with the tens of thousands of people across the world who buy *Collective Hub* every issue – and love it.

I firmly wanted to believe that, thanks to our untraditional business model (built on multiple revenue avenues rather than based purely on print advertising), we could outplay the game. As mentioned before, that we were not 'the media' but rather we were a movement. But, it seemed the evidence was stacking up against us, as the closures kept on coming. And we sadly weren't immune from some of the more traditional aspects of revenue raising such as advertising and partnerships – which, although they were increasing rather rapidly for my personal brand, were rapidly decreasing at a similar rate for *Collective Hub*. This was never the intention, and this could be an entire other book on personal brand vs. company. Trust me – I never MEANT to build myself as a brand – it just happened.

In the midst of my hardest periods with *Collective Hub*, Pacific Magazines in Australia laid off all but three of their 22 subeditors. Earlier that week, they'd announced 11 other redundancies. Meanwhile, Nick Chan left Bauer Media as CEO after little more than a year. And, Avant Card, Australia's first postcard advertising company, closed its doors, blaming the effect of digital advertising, social media and funding cuts to the arts.

In July, 2017 I received an email from Magshop, which at the time managed our reader subscriptions. It explained their "longer-term strategic decision" to "withdraw from the subscription fulfilment management business" at a date to be confirmed in the second quarter of 2018. Due to declining subscription volumes across the industry, along with fixed cost pressures and magazine closures, they believed the sector was no longer sustainable. So, another one hits the skids. It felt like a daily occurrence. Mice were deserting the sinking ship of print media everywhere we looked and, even someone as optimistic (and stubborn!) as me had days when I wondered if we could really be the exception.

As I edited this book, new figures from the Standard Media Index showed print magazines had seen a 42.5 per cent drop in ad bookings from media agencies in the past year, while print newspapers showed a 36.4 per cent drop. It seemed, no matter how incredible your contents, and how much readers loved you, budgets were tightening rapidly.

On the plus side, we were certainly making an impact. So often my team and I get emails, comments on social media, etc, etc, saying that *Collective Hub* has paved the way in editorial content and design. This, from start-ups across a myriad of industries, and from well-seasoned entrepreneurs, designers and creatives who almost use us to set trends, and universities who use our brand as a strong case study. While the print mag has not been a profitable pillar of the business, it has been one of the most important by far. In a largely digital age, having something physical and tangible made us stand out. And I wouldn't change any of it. Not for a second.

I'm so proud we supported an industry that people said was dying and did our bit to resuscitate it, even in the short-term. I'm incredibly proud that we inspired other print magazines to emerge into the marketplace, from university students who've told me they were inspired by us to launch a uni zine, to other independent magazines launched by solo female founders. I took every launch as a compliment.

When I launched, I got on the board of the industry association, Publishers Australia. I spoke at the national publishing conference three years in a row and in 2017 was the only Aussie invited to speak at the FIPP World Congress in London.

I'm proud that when so many other traditional 'actual' publishers were really struggling, we held the banner high for everyone espousing the importance of print and, I guess in a way, giving them all hope that anything is possible. After all, if some little punk like me who knew nothing about it could do it, surely we could all lift each other higher.

If I could go back, I'd still launch a print magazine every time, over and over – despite the naysayers who said digital was the only way forward. I'd still buck the trend, shake up the status quo and follow my gut instincts. I'd still prioritise creating a beautiful product that can be held in your hand, because I don't think our community would have fallen in love, so strongly, with a few words on a screen as they did our tangible – and aesthetically awesome – medium. But now, going against the tide was putting us in danger of sinking. How do you stay buoyant? How do you avoid being dragged down by naysayers, and instead adapt and pivot to survive? When all of your competitors are admitting defeat, or quietly drowning, is that a sign you should keep going? Or, do you need to think seriously about an exit strategy or alternative avenue –

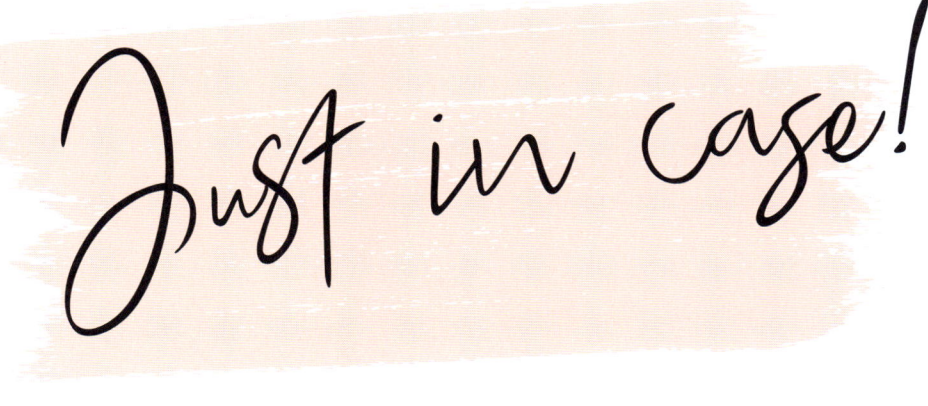

Just in case!

*

Trust the wait,
enjoy the uncertainty,
there is beauty
in not
Knowing

– ANON

We asked...

CAMILLA FRANKS

Camilla Franks is the founder of the Camilla fashion empire which has grown to become a global business with a celebrity client-base.

HOW HAVE YOU BUILT RESILIENCE?

"Any businesswoman will tell you a story or two about resilience. I have a whole library. Resilience comes hand in hand with launching, building, nurturing and fighting for your business. It also comes into play when facing the all-too-familiar vulnerability of being taken advantage of in a new venture.

One of my earliest lessons was to never be afraid to challenge. I got that from my producer days. That invaluable lesson has come into play with deadlines, budgets and negotiating – never taking no for an answer and never backing down in the face of a challenge.

My wild road trip to Camilla has been bumpy, and I've learnt a few lessons (often the hard way). My personality type is often resilient, but I naturally have a fear of failure. When you put every part of your heart and soul into something, it's easy to fall into the trap of feeling like a failure or losing your spark of courage, especially when you're a creative.

But courage is not without fear – it is the willingness just to show up no matter how you feel inside. It changes us and makes us a little bit stronger. I've stared rejection in the face countless times, but I refused to accept it. It has made me stronger and fight harder. I've walked my own path and one that is mine and mine only.

The result of that resilience is the Camilla you see today. It's our wholesalers who stock it and the loyal tribe of customers who wear it."

Are you positive?

To me, one of the biggest dangers to your self-belief isn't naysayers from outside your company – it's naysayers within your own team. I'm extremely lucky that, throughout my businesses, I've also seemed to attract the most incredible, optimistic, go-getting, anything-is-possible kinds of people. But everyone, especially when they suspect their job is on the line, can have a lapse of faith. It happens to the best of us, and to the best employees.

I've spoken to fellow entrepreneurs about this problem and how contagious a negative attitude is within a small (or large) company. It only takes one person to spark a conversation about the dire state of the industry and suddenly morale across your entire team drops. I've seen it, I've heard it and I'm quick to stop this kind of toxic talk before it does any kind of permanent damage.

In my own office, one certain member of staff would frequently say to me, "We're in SUCH a tough industry." It was their excuse for every situation – when sales dropped, if a cover concept didn't come off, if a partnership didn't happen. It just about drove me nuts, because that is such old-school thinking (which is one of the reasons this member of the team wasn't with us for very long before we parted ways).

When I heard this staff member complain that the industry is tough and that we didn't have "robust enough" numbers and stats to impress advertisers or potential partners, I wanted to throw my hands in the air and scream.

"We have SO many assets now," I wrote in my journal, after another frustrating meeting with this employee. "Way more than we've ever had, so I despise this excuse-based attitude. For goodness sake, we sold AU$200,000 worth of ads eight months out from launch, when no one had ever heard of me, everyone said print was dead or dying and we didn't even have a product yet. Now we have print, digital, social, events and on and on it goes. Now you look me in the face and tell me we have nothing to sell. I call big fat BS on that!!" But then again, maybe we just weren't moving at the speed and truly creating what advertisers and partners wanted to buy anymore.

This is a controversial view, but I think the same applies to the notion of the glass ceiling in many industries (although I know in some sectors it's a tangible problem). Whenever the notion of equality is raised in my staff meetings, I say at least 50 f*cks. It's not that I'm anti-equality. I just hate the word and, in many cases, see it as a non-issue. We give too much air-time to people complaining they couldn't achieve because of their gender, when actually it's sometimes a fear-based excuse and a 'poor me' mentality.

In 15.5 years of business I've never once felt I have fewer opportunities because I'm a woman. Now I know this is just my experience and that's not the same for some. But I am only qualified to talk about my truth. The same applies to the 'tough industry' argument. When I entered this industry I knew absolutely nothing, yet I sold a product that didn't even exist, approaching corporates for partnership deals with just a few pieces of paper and a passionate proposal.

Now *Collective Hub* was in year five, we could sit around the office dwelling on the state of media or realise that, despite the challenges, we were still standing strong and staying true to our ethos. Plus, even during our toughest times, we had CONSTANT victories, reasons to be grateful and achievements to celebrate.

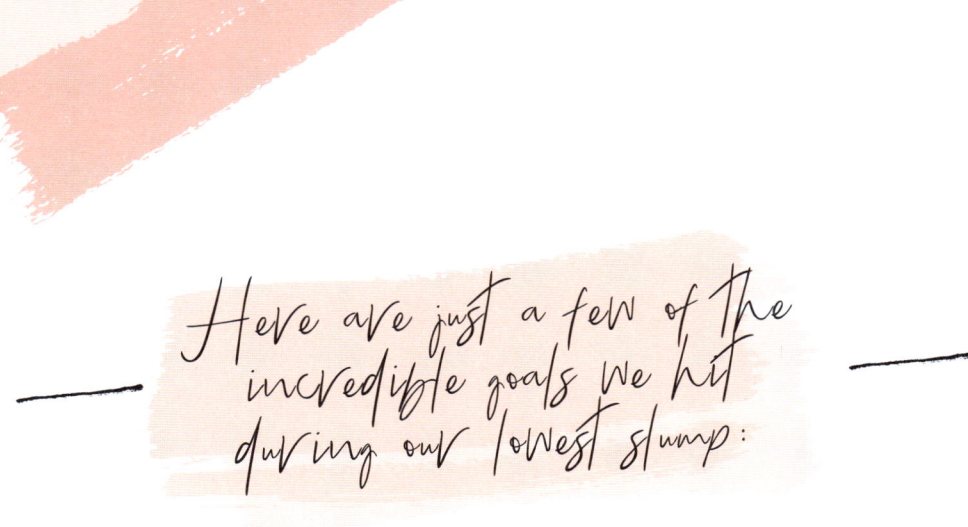

Here are just a few of the incredible goals we hit during our lowest slump:

X   We opened the Collective Retreat, a home-away-from-home for our community near Byron Bay where anyone looking for a creative retreat can escape the city to unwind, reboot and enjoy a vacation (or working holiday) in an incredible property, decorated by *Collective Hub*'s favourite designers and interior start-ups.

X   We got onto the radar of car manufacturers – a notoriously tough industry to secure advertising from unless you're a car magazine. One morning I received a AU$200,000 brief from a car company who were "dying to work with us". It seemed to open a floodgate and suddenly we had multiple car brands booking into our pages and across our digital and social assets.

X   Our Masterclasses went off! We couldn't keep up with demand for our expert talks in Sydney and so decided to start hosting them in Melbourne, Brisbane, Byron Bay, Perth and San Francisco, too. Wherever the location, they were consistently a sell-out. Plus, we struck contra deals with venues so the overheads were minimal. And the feedback from our community was incredible.

✗   Coles conducted an internal range review and, after sadly losing some titles, *Collective Hub* was given an increase from 136 stores to 633 stores. It did involve a stock reshuffle so that we didn't sell out in prime areas, but it skyrocketed our ranging across the country. That's an extra 497 shops stocking us in Australia!

✗   The launch of *Collective Hub*'s co-working space caused a huge stir and proved, once again, that people DO crave 'real world' connection and to feel part of an inspiring community. Although we ended up closing the space due to our move, the concept was a huge success during the time it was running (and could definitely re-emerge in the future).

✗   We managed to reduce general operating expenses by 27 per cent year-on-year (2017 versus 2016). Every entrepreneur will know this figure is no small feat and is an absolute credit to Damian and my CFO, who helped me mastermind our scale-down, and to my remaining staff who embraced every change that was thrown at them (mostly – they're only human!)

✗   My 2017 book release, *Purpose*, launched with incredible presales. Honestly, I am grateful for every person who ever buys any of my books and never take their success for granted. Although this book, *Risk & Resilience*, is probably the closest to my heart – because it's the most revealing insight into my life – but the topic of how to find your purpose was perfectly on point for our community, and I'm so thankful it hit a nerve with so many of you.

With every one of these victories I made sure we stopped to celebrate, even if it was just a 'well done team' group email, or a takeaway hamburger lunch on the balcony. Part of the reason I'm able to keep believing as a founder is because every month, every week, every day I have reminders. I'd go to an amazing press launch with the Spell girls in Byron Bay and meet 20 people who said *Collective Hub* saved them. Or, I'd get an email from an editor of one of the biggest magazines in the country, saying she LOVED our mag and did I have any vacancies?

One of my most heart-lifting emails was from Jonathan Mildenhall, at the time the CMO of Airbnb, who first opened a copy of *Collective Hub* on a flight between San Francisco and Sydney, when we interviewed him for an article.

"Initially I was planning a 40-minute flick," he wrote. "That's about right for a glossy you don't have a relationship with, right? No! Wrong! Some two-and-a-half hours later, having read nearly every profile piece within it, I turned back to the front cover.

I'm blown away by how your magazine makes me feel. Inspired. Empowered. Connected. Resourceful. Excited. Creative. Curious. Human. I didn't realise that my reservoir of creativity and humanity was running low until now. Now I feel it is overflowing with ideas and insight."

I'm happy to say feedback like this flooded in frequently. I have a huge stockpile of emails like this I can dip into when I wonder, on the rare occasion, if all the effort and money is worth it (answer: always YES!)

Unfortunately, your staff, when they're nose-down at their desks, don't always get these morale boosters and pick-me-ups. It's no wonder that doubt can creep into their minds, especially when the newspapers are so full of doom, gloom and industry closures.

My point? While you're busy plotting how to disrupt a crumbling industry, make sure the industry isn't crumbling your company – from the inside out. The best strategies are nothing without self-belief, determination and a collective can-do attitude. And, in times of crisis, they can be the first to fall.

> The best strategies are nothing without self-belief, determination and a collective can-do attitude. And, in times of crisis, they can be the first to fall

Rejoin the new class

In July, 2017, I vividly remember reading the new edition of *The Monthly* with Mark Zuckerberg on the front cover. The powerful coverline was, 'Killing Our Media'. In the article, it revealed Facebook's latest financial figures: "Total revenue soared by 49 per cent in the past year and profits topped $1 billion per month."

In May on the same day that Facebook announced its first-quarter earnings, Fairfax Media cut 125 editorial staff. That same month, literally hundreds, if not thousands of other redundancies were made across Australian and global media. In the article it stated, "This is what passes for normal marketing behaviour in 2017: news organisations, haemorrhaging under the costs of producing news while losing advertising, are paying the very outfits that are killing them. Could there be a more direct expression of the twisted relationship between them?"

In a way the article had a point. The interesting thing is that every single one of us who own the media is PUMPING money into Facebook advertising to boost our posts and to drive traffic to our organisation. At *Collective Hub*, we budget thousands upon thousands of dollars every month for Facebook advertising. But do I begrudge it? No! In fact, I find the relationship between old and new media fascinating.

I could have read that article and launched into a bitter tirade on social media. 'See! Facebook is KILLING US.' But what would that achieve for me, really? I would be a hypocrite to criticise ANYONE who is disrupting any industry, even if it has a negative effect on my own. Whether you're a taxi driver who hates Uber, a hotel whose lost out to Airbnb, or a movie theatre threatened by Netflix,

you can either complain about the new guard of completion or learn from them…
and move even FASTER.

Look at Polaroid who, despite printed photos falling from fashion, have pivoted
into focusing on "cameras for the digital age", including smartphones and tablets,
after selling their last instant Polaroid factory to The Impossible Project. They
even produced a 3D pen, which allows people to turn their photographs into
three-dimensional models.

Another example comes from the fashion industry. Rather than admit defeat
to online shopping, clever retail brands are installing tablets in their stores so
that customers can shop 'with one click' while in a retail environment.

The not-for-profit sector is also learning from the 'enemy'. After mental health
organisations realised the addictive power of technology and its downsides, they
began developing apps and games that ease anxiety and depression in young
people. Virtual reality games are helping soldiers deal with trauma and live apps
are connecting school children to counsellors. Instead of blaming gadgets for
adolescents' emotional unease, they're also becoming the antidote.

The same can happen in any industry. Most certainly, it is a massively
challenging time for media, but that kind of excites me, invigorates me and
inspires me. I just need a little time and space to figure out my next move… and
being in constant survival mode is not the place from which to do this. As I love
to say, let curiosity be your guide – you never know where it may lead you.

As *Collective Hub* emerged from catastrophe and began to break even, I was
able to stop and take a breath; read more, learn more and understand more.
Instead of blaming 'news feed media', I let myself become amazed by it, which
is a far more powerful mindset than resentment or anger. I realised we could lead
the charge if I just educated myself and my team to this new environment. So we
continued to get smaller. And leaner. And smarter. While still delivering a promise
to our community. Not easy to be doing more with less. But we did it and I'm so
proud of my team at the time.

As I wrote in *Daring & Disruptive*, "Entrepreneurs are the new heroes – running wildly towards their goals whilst their competitors watch in awe and, at times, fear." Now, at this crucial point for *Collective Hub*, it was time to take my own advice and revisit my own big, bold statements.

Around this time, someone close to me was in the process of developing a new business idea, after selling his very successful start-up. He'd been phenomenal at the planning process and ideating a new creative path around what he loves in life, the gap in the market and the possible tech play. It made me think about my own purpose and the larger, braver picture for *Collective Hub*… or, more bravely, was it *Collective Hub* at all OR a complete reinvention?

In any industry you have to keep moving, staying relevant, bucking the trend and keeping ahead of the curve or, in this day and age, you will implode. That didn't mean we had to stick to Plan A. This is why I'm not open to the "tough industry" commentary. Because, we're not just in the media industry – we're in whatever industry we morph into on that day, whether it's events, digital development or any other medium. If you're a start-up in a crumbling industry, remember this, always. When you have a kick-arse brand it can form the base for anything you want it to be. So be unafraid to get small, nimble and ready for phase 2.0.

Through all the conversations I had with potential buyers, so many people said they'd definitely invest in my NEXT idea – but didn't believe *Collective Hub* in its current form was sustainable, because print media is failing… and we didn't quite yet have the tech pivot.

This is true. Perhaps they had a point… I won't let ANYONE criticise the incredible brand identity we created or our overarching purpose. But the medium? How long could I ignore the fact that advertising dollars were dropping and some of our most loyal brands seemed to want to partner with me – Lisa Messenger the brand – rather than invest in the print magazine? One night, I spoke to a friend – one of my best friends – on the way home from the office and he said something like, "Oh don't try so hard – just let it collapse if it's meant to!" Man, that got my goat! Now, I am all for surrender and detachment from outcome but f*ck me. I've said this before – IF I let it crumble it would be a far HARDER path than it is now. You simply CANNOT walk away from something like this. I nearly screamed at him. Seriously! Can you even imagine? What would that mean? Probably months and months of liquidators and administrators and nightmare after nightmare. Not to mention the responsibility I have to my team members, our contributors and our wider community. No, that's not an option – period! The only option is to move forward and hopefully upwards.

As it turns out, this conversation was one of many in that 18 months (or even a five-year period) that led me to where I am now… he wasn't entirely wrong when he essentially said 'let it burn,' but I'd light my own fire and fan it my way. And I'd do everything responsibly and set up with dignity and grace fully intact.

Ironically, a few weeks after one of the big media companies said they couldn't invest in us, an article about how to come back from a 'no' appeared on their website, written by a freelancer, with a quote from lil' old me. I had given the writer an interview long before we approached them and were rejected. I laughed out loud when I read my quote, and realised the irony of where it was reported. "You know the cliché – one door closes and another opens," I'd said, not talking about investment but doors closing in my past. "In my experience, that new one is often so much bigger, more exciting and wonderful than you could have ever imagined." How BRILLIANT – and truer than ever!

I had to take the positives from the situation, and see it as an incredible test and a change to elevate *Collective Hub* to new heights. How do you make a brand that people love even more relevant, and by doing so, financially sustainable?

A funny story to end on… In my last book, *Purpose*, I wrote about the 'red box' in my office – a symbolic mind trick I accidentally created one day. A few years into the *Collective Hub* journey, I kept getting this feeling we were missing a piece of the puzzle and not yet serving a specific need of our community.

I couldn't put my finger on exactly what was missing, but the feeling was really sticky. So, I decided to draw an empty red box on the wall of my office, among my scribbled brainstorms and vision boards. I didn't put any pressure on myself to fill it with an answer; I just allowed it to rest a while amid my other crazy musings.

Within 24 hours the most extraordinary things started happening – I had three unexpected meetings with three unexpected people, who all suggested a similar avenue to venture down. THAT is the power of visualisation and manifestation.

Fast-forward 18 months and the red box appeared again – in a way that I couldn't avoid it! In November, 2017, I was driving over the Anzac Bridge back from the dentist when, at the last minute, I spotted something in the middle of the road – a red bucket. Going with the old adage, 'If there's a kangaroo in the middle of the road, don't swerve,' I hit it head on.

Now, unexpectedly, said red bucket wedged itself squarely under my car and stayed with me for the duration of the trip, making THE most horrendous noise. As I drove through the city, every time I stopped in traffic, people kept pointing and banging on the window, saying, "You have a red bucket under your car!"

Now, I'm a big one for believing in signs and serendipity. I didn't think of it at the time, but 24 hours later, when I was retelling that story, I realised it was perhaps a big wake-up call and shout from the universe. I remembered I had recently rubbed the red box off my wall. Never stop searching for undiscovered possibilities – or the universe might give you a sign you can't avoid.

Every challenge is a chance to practice resilience.

Be grateful

@LISAMESSENGER

AN OPEN LETTER TO CORPORATES

Dear Corporate World,
If you love us, support us!

Here's a typical interaction I have on a typical week in the office...
A global company gets in touch. They want to fly me to their
headquarters in Silicon Valley to visit their 'innovation laboratory'.
It sounds amazing but, as I tell them, we already sent my previous
editor to visit their headquarters. We've run more than 20 stories on
this brand in the magazine. We've gone out of our way to champion
them, because I truly believe in their vision.

...And you haven't spent a cent with us. Yet I see you spending
with others.

I'll give you another example of a similar situation. The head of HR
for one of the Big Four business auditors asks to meet me for lunch.
She apparently has more than 100,000 staff under her remit. She says
Collective Hub is her "bible" and my books have guided her business
strategy. Yet, when I ask if she'd consider bulk-buying copies of the
magazine to gift her teams, she says it's just not possible.

The same goes for a certain bank that I've been talking to for five
years. They won't advertise but they do keeping inviting me to lunch to

talk about "opportunities". When I emailed their brand manager to suggest Collective Hub might in the future be changing direction, they were shocked. "Oh no, but why?"

Because, we're going under if you don't support us!

While I was sitting at the airport the other day, in one hour I received seven emails from companies asking for us to do a story on them — three from complete start-ups but four from very well-established, businesses who wanted us to talk about their huge successes and growth.

As we've done more than 6000 stories and are showcasing so many people with little in return, I thought I would do a quick experiment. I emailed all seven back and asked what their marketing or advertising budget was to support the particular campaign they were talking about. Every single one of them emailed back and said that oh no — there was no marketing budget. Now... this is where there is a big problem. A disconnect. And one that breaks my heart.

For so long we have been showcasing brands, telling amazing stories and sharing people's voices to inspire other people. Yet people do not seem to realise that if we aren't supported financially, then there simply won't BE a media platform and outlet to showcase all these amazing stories for free.

It's time to call corporates out, for the sake of the start-up scene. Every day we get emails from people from all walks of life, verticals and industries saying, 'You changed my life'. Well, stop making it so hard for us to work with you — and be paid for it.

The irony is it's the smaller brands who have supported us. A tiny footwear company is happy to give us AU$8000 for an ad, over and over again, even though they have no money, I'm sure. Yet a banking giant can't muster AU$12,000 for three adverts at a special discount. Are you serious???

How do you think we produce this incredible magazine every two months (and almost every month for four years prior)? A magazine that inspires you, revives you, delights you and steers the direction of your business which, according to reports, brings in millions?

We are fighting on, but time is running out.

If you love us, stand by us — loyally and financially.

With love,
The Start-up Community
X

Every next level of your life will demand a different version of you

Chapter Nine

Stepping into your genius zone

CHAPTER NINE

Stepping into your genius zone

When things seem insurmountable and you have endless questions about the future, sometimes the best thing you can do is step away from it all, even though it may seem like a crazy thing to do when working 24/7 feels like it should be the answer. This is exactly what I did in January, 2018 after my partner suggested we spend the entire month in Bangalow, at the Collective Retreat near Byron Bay.

When he first made the suggestion I thought he was insane. Do you know what's going on inside my business at the moment? I need to be there, plotting, pushing, strategising and reconstructing. But the more I thought about it, it felt like an increasingly sensible option.

At the time, everyone was pushing me from every direction – the M&A guys, our consultants, my team, our clients. Everyone wanted answers, decisions and solutions. And everyone wanted them IMMEDIATELY. "Guys, the only way I can make decisions is to stop the noise," I told my team who, thankfully, were only too happy to support me.

From the moment I arrived in Byron Bay I made a very conscious, very clear and determined decision. As I've shared in my previous books, my self-care routines – whether it's swimming in the ocean, eating healthy foods or doing yoga – have always supported me, through loss, heartbreak, breakdowns and breakthroughs. So, while I was away from the office – and away from 'normality' – I made a vow to be insanely ritualistic.

I buried myself in a routine that enlivened me, inspired me and rebooted me. Don't get me wrong – this was still a working holiday. I structured my work around healthy, nurturing pillars. Every day I got up at 5.55am, had a green smoothie and did a Barre Body or yoga class. These became my non-negotiables.

Then, sitting in a café, I listened to an inspiring or educational podcast. And THEN I started working, even though my to-do list was still never-ending. We finished every day with a walk and beach swim, and no technology – especially email-checking (even when I was waiting to hear feedback from investor meetings).

There are many myths around productivity which we've all been tricked into believing; you have to work 9-5, you have to sit at the desk, you're more productive in an office and self-care should be 'fitted in' before or after your work hours. But anyone who has given themselves permission and freedom to work in their own way will testify that there's no one more productive, creative and inspired than an entrepreneur in flow. And, to be in flow you have to find space to step into your 'genius zone'.

Your Genius Zone – the magical mental space where ideas flow, creativity wakes you up with excitement and no problem or issue can manage to dampen your brightness.

You can find your genius zone anywhere – in a bustling office, in the back of a taxi, at an airport when your flight is delayed by six hours. But, more likely than not, the greatest lightbulb moments occur when you move away – mentally or physically – from the constant tug and pull of life's commitments. The idea for *Collective Hub* came about in the first place after I gave myself space and time to ask the universe, "How can I be of service?" I prayed, visioned, manifested over a matter of months and years. More importantly, I didn't try to rush or force the answer.

Going to Byron was the third time since launching *Collective Hub* where I'd reached a dead-end creatively, and had to leave normal life behind to find a solution. In October, 2016, I went to India in meltdown mode. I was in a bad place (possibly, quite luckily, I didn't realise how bad at the time). For 11 days, I immersed myself in a meditation centre and emerged with a new energy and clarity about my future.

Before this, in January, 2016, I'd gone to Bali for a trip that turned into a life-changing vacation, when I visited an orphanage and fell in love with a little girl called Gracie who melted my heart and inspired my own journey to have a baby. Few people, apart from my nearest and dearest confidants know about the two rounds of IVF with a donor that I had undergone, alone, while running *Collective Hub*, before meeting the incredible man I hope I'm destined to parent with.

The opposite of giving yourself space is accidentally scheduling an IVF cycle around the busiest work week of the year. In a 24-hour period I flew to New Zealand for a speaking gig for 1200 people, got back on a plane and went straight on stage to co-host the Virgin Way Conference with Sir Richard Branson, then the following day got on a plane to spend the weekend at Makepeace Island. All the while I was carrying around my little bag of needles and syringes with my makeshift freezer bag.

So, you could say I've experienced the two sides of the equation – what happens when you give yourself space and freedom to thrive. And, what happens when you squash your dreams with commitments, responsibilities and reactiveness.

An amazing entrepreneur I know, who sold his start-up for tens of millions before moving on to equally amazing things, said he felt like he was locked in a cage for the longest time. Even when you love your company, I can see how this feeling would creep up on you. After selling his start-up, he spent 30 days hiking along the Camino trail – almost 1000 kilometres. This was around the time *Collective Hub* was at its most fragile. I couldn't help but envy his freedom and that sense of escapism.

That's why I knew that, as a new year dawned for *Collective Hub*, I had to step away to step forward. To start 2018 strongly, I had to consciously reset; responding without being reactive, let go and get back into the flow, to enable me to step up to a completely different level. To get still. To be. To surrender.

When I got back to the office everyone said, "How was your holiday?" It wasn't a holiday! It was a reboot. And thank goodness I took it. Otherwise, I might not have discovered the strength, clarity and courage to make the boldest decision of my entrepreneurial life to date –

and step back into joy!

*

— How to retreat yourself —

Okay, I know we can't all run away to Byron Bay. But it is possible to access your genius zone at home. When you can't get away, go within...

✗ BLUR YOUR BOUNDARIES

Sometimes as a founder it is necessary to work weekends. It can actually cause you more stress to ban work and know that it's building up for Monday. Instead, find ways to mix business and pleasure ('bleisure!'). One memorable weekend, I met a member of our advisory board for a lovely two hour walk. We kicked goals and got an endorphin boost, too.

✗ GET GROUNDED

Anyone who follows my Instagram account knows I am a bit obsessed with plants – especially cacti! One of my most relaxing rituals is planting and propagating. I can lose an entire weekend to this earthing activity. Even better if you can convince friends to help you with the digging and combine a bit of 'eco-therapy' with an uplifting social activity. Break from your 'story'. At one point, every day I felt completely whacked, as I was telling the *Collective Hub* story and our vision over and over to potential partners, working out creative ways to work together. Even when you love it, talking about yourself – or your start-up – constantly can be draining. That's why I value the time I spend with friends who aren't in the start-up space, talking about anything and everything ASIDE from business.

✗ FEED YOUR CURIOSITY

In Byron Bay, I listened to a lot of Tim Ferriss and Oprah's SuperSoul Conversations, alongside every episode of the How I Built This podcast. Whatever your appetite, find ways to educate yourself, inspire yourself and increase your knowledge bank. The lessons come thick and fast when you're open to them and willing to become a student again.

✗ DON'T TAKE IT PERSONALLY

Stop obsessing about what other people think of you – it really is that simple. You can choose, from today, to stop being hung up on other people's expectations. This doesn't mean you stop caring or stop seeking outside opinions. But return to your gut feeling as a guide rather than external influences. Then watch your energy flood back in.

The
GENIUS
ZONE

Where ideas flow,
creativity abounds
and anything is
possible

@LISAMESSENGER

After the adrenalin wears off

You may not have realised that I've been writing this book in real time. Unlike many books written about events that happened to the author a year ago, decade ago or lifetime ago, as I type this, *Collective Hub*'s hardest year isn't a distance memory – it's my current reality. It was a conscious decision to share my story with you as it happens. It's easy (or far easier) to look back on events in the past and see the positive lessons you can take away from them.

But I wanted to share my experience in all its rawness and realness while I lived it, breathed it and was still strapped into the rollercoaster. To truly be able to help other people going through a similar experience, I knew I had to write as I was in it (as I have done with my previous five books in this series). This way, I would be 100 per cent tuned into advice that I wish I'd been given when it was happening.

This is where I have to be honest. When I started writing this book, I thought it would have a very different ending. When I began typing the introduction and plotting out possible chapter headlines, I thought the fairytale ending would be finding an investor or, at the most dramatic, selling the business completely. That's why the title of this book was, *Risk & Resilience: from Start-up to Survival to Scale Up*. It then became *Survival to Exit*. And, then back to *Scale Up* again. Keep up!

As I sit here right now, I'm facing a very different reality. We have now been in Byron for 20 days, and it is the single most important thing I could have done for me, for *Collective Hub* and for my personal relationship.

For the first time in forever, I actually spent an entire day just considering, 'What does the future of Lisa Messenger look like and how can I best serve the planet?' Since the day I launched *Collective Hub,* I have stated loudly and proudly that I believe my purpose is "to be an entrepreneur for entrepreneurs, living my life out loud and showing that anything is possible". The purpose of *Collective Hub* is to "ignite human potential". I do not believe my purpose has changed. Not one little bit.

But there is also a very important, although slightly terrifying question, that every entrepreneur needs to keep asking themselves, bravely and courageously: 'Is THIS my greatest calling now. Is THIS channel still the best to serve my community?'

This was brought home to me recently when we launched our Digital Masterclass series. It was a big decision – and a HUGE project for my team – to turn our very popular Collective 101 Masterclasses into an online version that is accessible to anyone, anywhere. We kept getting feedback from people who couldn't attend an event, because of their geographical location, but kept hearing about them and felt they were missing out on an education.

So, over the course of two incredible days, I put my thoughts onto film, working with an incredible videographer, under the guidance of my watchful team. We offered the first Digital Masterclass, How to Pitch to the Media, at a special discounted rate to our community for 24 hours – and the response was PHENOMENAL.

Along with my digital marketing manager, on the night that we launched we watched the comments pop up on the portal, from people who'd bought the masterclass and already viewed it. "Thank you for putting this together. You and your team constantly amaze me." "This is so powerful. Before watching, I didn't think my story was that special or interesting. Now, I feel differently." "Funny how we stumble across things… this is just what I need right now." "It often astounds me how the universe aligns. This popped up on my newsfeed at the perfect time. Talk about a sign!" We had responses from people across all different industries – founders of tech start-ups, not-for-profits, innovators in the medical world, inventors and creatives. People who, for a long time, wanted to get their story out into the world but didn't have the confidence, courage, resources or know-how to share their dreams, their achievements and their aspirations.

That night, I couldn't stop thinking about work – in a good way! Here was an army of people who, if it wasn't for our latest launch, would go un-serviced. A community seeking guidance and support who had been restricted, in the past, from attending our 'real world' events and so were at a disadvantage. If we hadn't pivoted our Masterclasses onto a different platform, and added online courses to our portfolio, they would still feel unsupported. That's the opposite of our inclusive ethos!

Yet, it would have been easy to put off producing these videos. In fact, we'd come up with the idea years ago, but put off actioning it because, before our scale-down we were just too busy running in circles, and after our scale-down, I didn't think we had the resources to produce them. It had pushed my team to their limits, producing the Digital Masterclasses at the same time as going to press on the latest issue of the magazine.

The rousing reaction from viewers instantly made me want to film MORE! There were so many topics that we could cover which would be beneficial to our community, and elevate and lift them higher. But, could I ask my team to stretch themselves even further? Could I spare the expense of the videography and editing process, over and over, when currently the 'hero product' of our business was only just breaking even – at best?

That is how I came to make a huge decision, that I never expected to be writing here when I began writing this book's introduction: "As of issue 52 of *Collective Hub*, the print magazine will be closing." Surprise – or not so much of a surprise if you're reading this after our announcement.

Believe me, it's not a decision I took lightly. As you know, I am the biggest champion of a tangible media product. I LOVE the feel of a magazine, I love

the rituals of flicking through pages, snapping pictures of quotes I love and then passing the edition onto friends I think will benefit.

As an author, I've always adored the power of words on paper. I'm the person with a big pile of magazines next to her sofa who tears pages out and sticks them onto her vision board.

This isn't the outcome I thought I'd be typing… but it's increasingly clear that I know it IS the best option. If our search for investment taught me anything, it's that we have a brand people love; a brand that, in some form, I have to protect for the future. I could probably keep the print magazine going in survival model for another five years. But at what cost? It would drain all of our spare resources and my personal savings (ha… who am I kidding, they were gone long ago); money and mental energy that we could use to do powerful things for our community.

And my promise from day one was to keep disrupting, reinventing, staying ahead of the game, bucking the status quo… so I need to honour that to be true to myself, our community and my purpose.

Sure, I lost a small fortune in many people's eyes BUT fricken' hell I had the biggest, most incredible, most amazing ride of my life for the past five years. I wouldn't change a bit of it. If that's what money has bought me – I would have paid 10 times that just for the experience. It's not about the money for me. It's never been about the money. It's about doing incredible things on this planet; having AMAZING experiences, living my best life, giving it my all, having a go and lifting others higher.

I am prepared to take a BIG financial hit in my life. But I'm not prepared to see everything we've worked for disappear. I'm also not prepared to grab just any investment opportunity in desperation and be buried in some media giant, swallowed up, our souls and very being left to die as the last skerrick of 'change the world' is squeezed out of us by some suit sitting in a beige boardroom. I realised this when a potential investor accidentally forwarded me an email

RISK & RESILIENCE

from her colleague saying, 'Is she dreaming? It's a mess,' talking about the state of my baby. That email left a bitter taste in my mouth and lit a fire in my belly! One of the most disappointing things about this email was the sender – a fellow businesswoman – who had previously said to my face that *Collective Hub* was one of the single biggest things that changed her life.

It goes back to the 'Open Letter to Corporates' that I shared in the last chapter. If you love us, support us! If you love us, stand by us! It made me remember just how much the start-up scene needs a strong community – a place, portal or platform that unites every single one of us who is constantly fighting the good fight to hold our own against the big guns.

I have realised more and more AND I am FINALLY taking a stand on this. I have attended SO many PR events over the past five years to support a number of BIG brands across a myriad of industries. However, more recently I've realised that a lot of the time it's a one-way street. We continue to sing the praises of brands across our social, digital and print platforms, yet few of these actually 'spend' with *Collective Hub*.

It has taken me a long time (because I'm a people-pleaser), but I have finally started saying no – and telling the truth as to why. As I told one (very profitable) brand, "We have supported your brand for the past five years. We often attend your events, we show you love, we cover you editorially. We watch you spending with other publications and media outlets, yet you never support us. I am putting an end to this and until you support us we will no longer be in a position to support you. Without your support *Collective Hub* may not exist soon. I am tired of the big brands taking advantage of smaller brands who are actually doing good and giving others a voice in the world."

I haven't heard back.

But it's true and, in retrospect, I should have taken this stance sooner – to stop supporting corporate brands that we feature all the time and never spend with us.

As a friend said, "Good call and I agree. No spend, no free love. It's not that kind of party!"

For now, back to the closure (or, at least, the hiatus) of the print magazine…

You might still ask, why do I need to 'break' *Collective Hub* and pause its original product, instead of just adding to it? Well, sometimes you can't just keep adding to the same business – it takes a loss or substitution to create new beginnings. I recently sat down with an entrepreneurial friend who sold his start-up for a phenomenal sum. He's currently in the process of ideating a bigger, bolder plan, which in many ways would have been the next logical step for his first company.

Why not just implement those plans within his other brand? Why did he feel the need to sell his baby and start over, to step into the next level? His reply, over email, held an incredible amount of insight. With his permission, I'll share it with you:

"I knew my time was up, not because I had lost my passion for what we were doing, but because I needed to start from the beginning again. It's difficult to explain but over time we add lawyers, we add sh*t, we create certain ways of doing things, we become slightly more pessimistic, we believe a little less and we accept compromises and justifications a little more.

"Sometime we even start to listen to our own little voices in our heads. And, most deadly of all, sometimes we allow ego to build up and we stop listening to our customers and start listening to our ourselves instead. We all become a little jaded, with time… that's inevitable, unfortunately. That's just what time does. That's why big companies suck, because over time… they just keep adding and adding and become bigger and bigger, slower and slower.

"I knew that I needed to scrap it all. I knew that I needed to stop to disrupt my thinking. Throw it all in the bin and start again. I needed to start with a fresh, blank, white piece of paper and start over."

That is, increasingly, how I'm beginning to feel about *Collective Hub*.

Not that I need to walk away completely, but that I need to begin clearing my canvas to make space to be able to begin creating – in multicolour.

Right now, the welfare of my team is my ultimate concern and that hasn't changed. With this decision, I'm not sure yet where they'll all land. But, as I have said before, they are all amazing and if a few people need to be re-homed (for a period while I have time and space to explore avenues) – hopefully in the new iteration of the business – then we will support them and do it with dignity and grace.

As I've said before, we could continue to struggle indefinitely – and my staff could go on working under a cloud of uncertainty – or I could move forward with some, and allow the others to be free, to go on to bigger, brighter and more stable opportunities.

As for me... Why not get out at the top and be strong enough to pivot? That's what a true entrepreneur does, and it's what we stand for. I could no longer ignore the fact the print magazine was holding us back. It also had finite restrictions – the number of magazines we can print, the numbers of stores that will stock us, the countries where we're not available due to the monstrous cost of importation. If I truly wanted to stay true to our mission – to ignite the potential of people, globally – I have to think outside the box, again. Or, in this case think outside our paper pages...

A true entrepreneur isn't limited by restrictions or expectations. They get a no and hear 'what's next?' They turn a bump into a bounce. They face every disappointment, every rejection, every change in direction with courage, resilience and a renewed determination to prove their naysayers wrong.

Closing the magazine isn't the easy option in any way. Even financially I stood to lose a LOT; paying back our subscribers and freelancers we'd commissioned for upcoming issues, plus over two years' worth of salary I haven't paid myself, and the personal money I've sunk into *Collective Hub*, not to mention certain staff members who wouldn't all be able to move forward with me.

But I also couldn't ignore the excitement I felt in my belly; the burst of adrenaline that always hits me before amazing things happen, and the overwhelming faith I felt that everything was exactly on track as it should be. As the founder of a magazine for game-changers, thought-leaders, risk-takers and style-makers, that has urged our community to dig deep, pivot with purpose and leap into the unknown, it was time I lived up to my words (again!).

✳

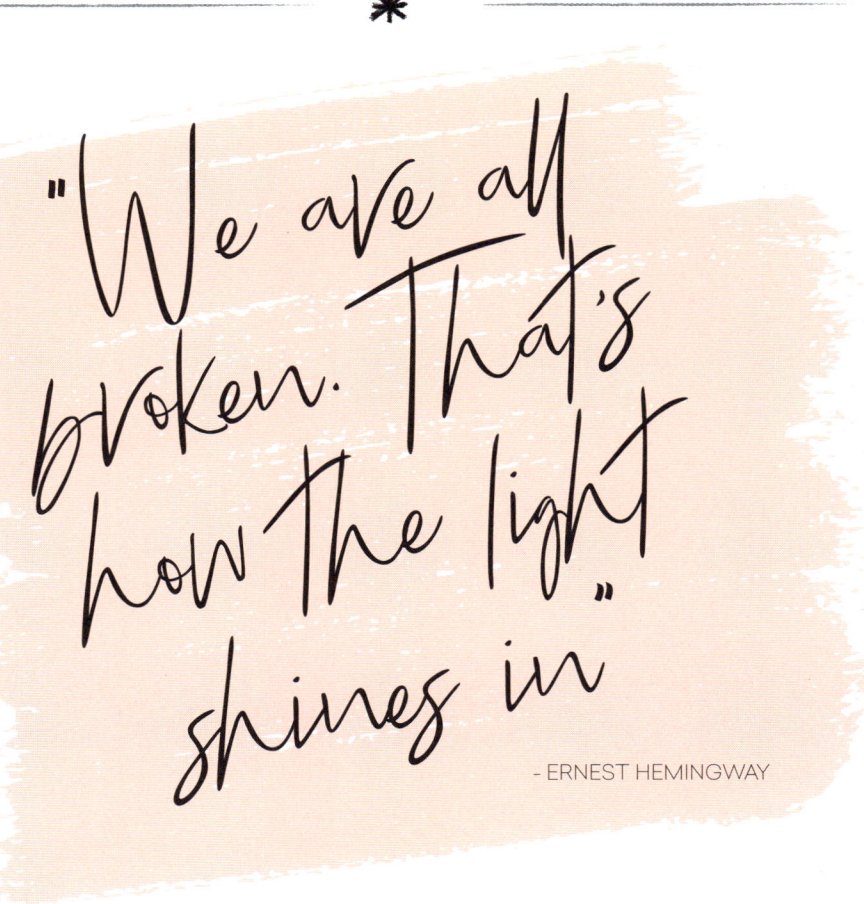

"We are all broken. That's how the light shines in"

— ERNEST HEMINGWAY

A REBEL'S GUIDE TO BUILDING RESILIENCE

✗ FLIP YOUR MINDSET
Constantly reframe, reposition and repurpose negative thoughts, feelings and situations into a positive possibility. Slow time in your business? Use it for long-term strategy. Meeting cancelled? Use that hour for a self-care ritual. It's far better than brooding.

✗ GET A NATURE HIT
Take a stroll around a park, go for a dip in the ocean or go and water the plants in your office (mindfully!). It's amazing what a tint of green will do to your day.

✗ USE SOCIAL MEDIA FOR GOOD
Yes, scrolling through other peoples' feeds can make you feel worse sometimes. But gravitate to someone's feed who always makes you smile, enlightens you or uplifts you. You know who they are!

✗ ASSESS YOUR SCHEDULE
Be aware of the impact of excess travel or commitments on your emotional state. Jet-lag, long-haul travel and too many public speaking gigs can cause me to nose-dive, mentally. Learn to say no!

✗ FAKE IT 'TIL YOU MAKE IT
There will be times, especially in the early days, when you don't feel strong, optimistic and eternally sunny. A meeting with a client is probably the last place you want to be, but you might find that, after an hour plugging the positives of your business, you believe your own hype again.

✗ DON'T BEAT YOURSELF UP FOR BAD DAYS
Even the most insanely resilient founder in the world (I'm up there!) has moments where they sob in their car (I've been there!). Don't make yourself feel worse by feeling like you've failed. Remember, tomorrow is a new day.

We _asked..._

EMMA SEIBOLD

Emma Seibold, co-founder of Barre Body and Bende, which combined have 10 thriving studios across Australia.

HOW CAN YOU RISE DURING YOUR TOUGHEST TIMES?

"As I write this, I am exhausted, spent and almost broken. After the hardest year of my life there isn't a lot in my tank, but it is precisely at this time that I need to reach down deep, deep, deep and find the reserves to put it all back together again. That is resilience.

My businesses, owned and managed jointly with my gorgeous husband, Matt – Barre Body and Bende – are thriving. My team however, is not. I'm about to catch it all just in time to stop things from falling apart, but it will be a close ran thing.

In late 2016, my beautiful mother was diagnosed with terminal pancreatic cancer and within seven months she died – at home, with me, my brother and my family caring for her. It was both very special and desperately, desperately sad. In the months after my mother died, I felt broken and unmoored – set adrift without my anchor or floating in space, untethered from the mothership. I was still whole, but the pieces were a little broken. Or as I also described it, I felt like a puzzle – all the pieces still there and in their right place, but just spread out and not quite put together.

Just four months later in October, 2017, I lost my only sibling, my brother, tragically and suddenly. If I were a little broken before, that experience truly broke my heart. But not, thankfully, my spirit. At that time, I felt an incredible strength and sense of being grounded, powerful and solid.

All throughout 2017 my incredible team rallied around me and pulled together to keep the Barre Body and Bende fires burning, engines running, classes full and clients happy, but as it turns out, without me holding them up and stoking their fires, they too fell apart. Not everyone and not completely, but enough for things to be pretty serious. They exhausted and burnt themselves out trying to look after me and our business. That in itself is a measure of our team's resilience and power, and perhaps even me as a leader.

But now, at a time when I am still grieving, still desperately sad, still exhausted, and still not quite put back together, I have to put my team back together and restore the incredible culture, positivity and energy we have in our businesses. I have to get my head back in the game and give it all I have (or, more accurately, all that's left after I care for my family – always my number one priority).

How does one do this? For me it starts with gratitude.

Gratitude for everything – from the sunshine, to electricity, to my children – but most importantly, immense gratitude for the challenges and heartbreaks, for they are what shape me, give me strength, and transform me into a deeper, fuller person.

Then it's love. It always comes down to love.

Recognising everyone's efforts and sacrifices and acknowledging them with love. Holding my team in love and reminding them that I am there to support them, grow them and nurture them. That the business they work in is a container to provide them with safety, security, and amazing, wonderful experiences that both fill them up and expand them to be even bigger and brighter than they were before.

This isn't the first challenge my business has faced and, please forgive the predictability of the statement, it certainly won't be the last. But to me, a challenge is simply an opportunity to rise up, become greater, and surpass where I was before. it's nice to be hungry again. Hunger makes me creative, inspired and alive."

Let go and flow

O ver the past 20 days I've been reading about the amazing entrepreneurs who've embraced the power of the pivot. Look at Ashton Kutcher who morphed from teen actor to venture capitalist and is now the founder of the incredibly charity, Thorn, which was set up to deal with the intersection of child sexual exploitation and technology.

I was fortunate enough to hear Ashton Kutcher speak and then meet him in Sydney a few years ago, when *Collective Hub* ran a story on his transition from actor to entrepreneur and angel investor. His knowledge, humility, selflessness and integrity blew me away then. And my opinion was only heightened when I heard him speak at the Dreamforce conference during our trip to San Francisco.

I have enormous respect for people like him who are not only able to build a platform (in his case, that of a celebrity movie star), but then traverse industries and use that platform for the power of good.

It's an important lesson for all of us. Once you've built a profile and a fanbase, you don't have to be pigeonholed. It's within your power to redirect your focus and your communities. Who would have thought the young, hippy guy from *That '70s Show* would grow into a 'digital defender of children'.

He's not the only 'high-profiler' to have done this. Angelina Jolie has become a human rights activist. Will.I.Am is now an innovator in the tech space, after moving from music into gadgets. The incredible popularity of Netflix has convinced some of the world's biggest movie stars to turn their back on Hollywood studios and instead work exclusively for an online streaming platform.

If you embrace change, rather than fearing it, then mind-blowing things can happen. Since *Collective Hub*'s launch we've covered countless amazing 'normal' people who've undergone incredible pivots and changed their purpose or platform: the fashion designer who set up a not-for-profit that provides wardrobes for women fleeing domestic violence, the divorce lawyers who created an app to soothe children whose parents are separating, the plus-sized model who has become an activist for eco-conscious living.

When you look outside the box and allow your purpose, your passion and your career to evolve and grow, the unimaginable can happen. This is something that all entrepreneurs have to remember before they pigeonhole themselves in one specific niche of one specific industry.

I have ALWAYS said, from day one of launching *Collective Hub*, that we are not about a print magazine. As an entrepreneur, don't worry too much about your delivery mechanism or your platform – it is largely irrelevant. Worry about your purpose and what you stand for.

With *Collective Hub* we have morphed through so many iterations from print to digital, social, events, video and masterclasses to co-working. Now it's time to find what is the next big way to disrupt and bring our purpose to life for as many people as possible, globally. My gut feel is a very big tech play...

I LOVE print media and can't say for certain that issue 52 was the last time you'll hold a print copy of *Collective Hub* magazine. I'm incredibly proud of the impact we had on the industry. Just last week I met with a designer who used to work for Typo and she said, "EVERYONE looks to you for inspiration." We made entrepreneurism cool! We also learnt, from scratch, how to create a magazine and nothing's stopping us doing it again if the industry goes full circle.

We have incredible relationships with the likes of NewsLink and WHSmith who have supported us beyond anything I could imagine. As have Coles and Woolies, alongside 3506 newsagencies in Australia and then all the outlets in another 37 or so countries... just WOW. While I've got your attention, a MASSIVE shout out to ALL of them. Our distributors have been there, by my side, every single step of the way. I'm sure the doors will still be open for *Collective Hub* to make a re-appearance on shelves in some form in the future, if we wish to. I firmly and faithfully believe *Collective Hub* is strong enough as a brand to transcend into new mediums – and leave irrelevant ones behind us. Every single member of my advisory board has said, "The print magazine and the current iteration of *Collective Hub* as a brand, this is JUST the foundation." When enough people say it, you have to trust that something bigger is going to happen.

One of the most liberating lessons you can learn as an entrepreneur is to know when to strip a brand down, when to step away, when to transition and when to create something bigger. While you cling onto the old – in our case a money-absorbing medium – you can't possibly make way for the next evolution.

It's a brave move to know when to call it and train yourself to know that there is something bigger around the corner. Too many people cling on to what they have and slowly but surely their business, their dream and their life and soul die and they lose everything.

I have incredible admiration for entrepreneurs who knew when to call it quits or change direction. Incredible stories of start-up pivots include Odeo turning into Twitter, Flickr which began as an online role-playing game called Game Neverending and Instagram which started life as Burbn, a check-in app that lets users make plans with friends and post pictures of their meet-ups (the part of the app that was most popular, as its founders discovered).

For every founder who has pivoted, there's another who clung on stubbornly to idea number one – and eventually lost everything. Loyalty and dedication to an idea is ESSENTIAL to being a successful entrepreneur, but so is the ability to constantly change, evolve and be a seeker of new opportunities. And, it's a hell of a fun journey! There is nothing more thrilling than the moment a new idea drops, which excites every cell of your body.

When you've been running the same start-up for multiple years, it can be easy to forget the incredible rush of early stage ventures. Think back to your brand's beginnings, when you couldn't WAIT to tell people about your plans, when brainstorming sessions were full of wonder, when every step was a novelty, and excitement overshadowed worries. The best part of pivoting is you get a whole new perspective, and can explore an entirely new landscape.

So, as I type this I don't have an exact ending to this story. For that I can't apologise, even though the traditional publishing industry would probably say I shouldn't publish this book without one (when have I ever been traditional?). Sometimes, on this entrepreneurial journey, chapter number nine ends up being just the beginning. And your hero product turns out to just be a sidekick, paving the way for a...

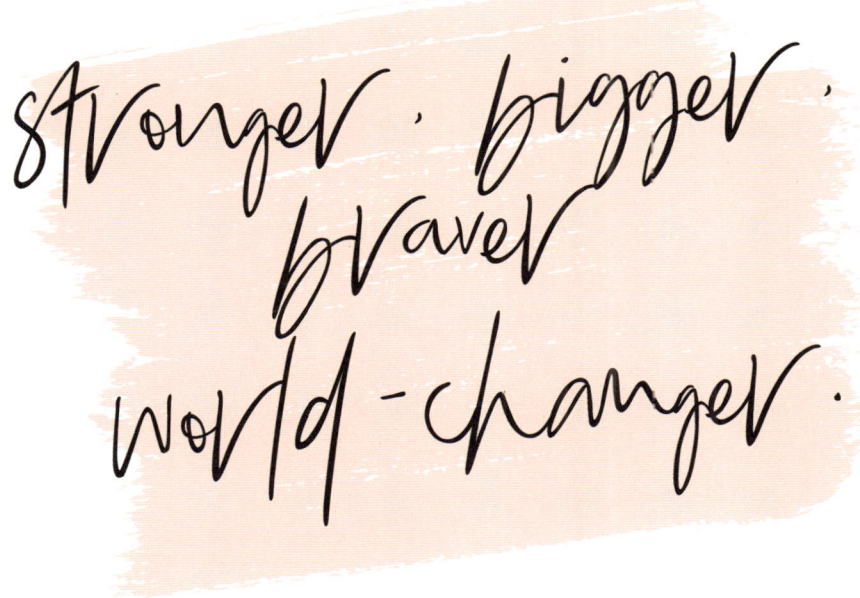

stronger, bigger, braver world-changer.

*

Money or your life

y the time you read this book, perhaps *Collective Hub* 2.0 or whatever form the new company takes will have fully manifested, or it may still be in the incubation phase. Even now, my mind is alive with possibilities, pivots and new iterations. It's time to go down a different path. It's time to move forward but also be still. It's time to tap into my unwavering purpose and ask again, "How can I be of service?" It's also time to look at the sacrifices I've made for the business and ask, how long can you continue to give, give, give before burn-out?

I've spoken in the past about the power of mindset, and how you can choose to flip your attitude to gratitude and, BOY, was the last 18 months a reminder. There have been brief moments when I've wondered if all the struggle could possibly suck the entrepreneurial spirit from me (I'm talking VERY brief moments when, after a horrendous day of meetings, I've sat in my car and sobbed until I had nothing left).

You might be in this situation now. I hope not, but I know I'm not the first – and certainly not the last – entrepreneur to be pushed to their brink in the pursuit of their purpose. That's why I have a VERY important message for anyone reading this, anyone wondering if they can really start over, if they can really go on, if they're really cut out for this life. YOU ARE! A bad patch is just that – a patch in your history. We've all been there. If you take anything from this book, make it that truth.

In months or years to come, when you have time and space between yourself and this period of intense survival, you'll feel bright again, light again and ready to disrupt again. For some, it might take a while, like my friend who hiked the Camino trail. For me, it truly only took those four weeks that I spent in Byron

Bay to feel like my old, rebellious, anything-is-possible self again. Despite everything, I found I WAS able to step into a big, disruptive mindset again; I was able to compartmentalise any recent disappointments, rejections, tough days and harsh emails from the amazing opportunities that were in front of me. To trust that the future is going to be bigger and better, and that I CAN choose to step into it. This is the most incredible test and lesson for every founder – the ability to trust the future while the past is grabbing at, and trying to choke and smother your dreams.

(For anyone struggling to nurture a mindset like this, I talk about ALL the tools I've built up over the years in my previous books. In fact, I re-read ALL of my own books during this time to take a dose of my own advice – and it worked).

I also gave myself space to remember my dreams OUTSIDE the business. Yes, it's okay to be a founder and still want more than success for your start-up. I was able to really remember that business is just business – a game we play that we may win or lose but must never take too seriously. Instead, I got serious about how I wanted the rest of my life to look – health, love, personal ambitions, motherhood, family, seeking, learning, exploring. And, although I was losing a piece of my business – and a big piece – by the end of my thought process my life has never felt so full.

This is not the story of a failed founder, although it could have been if I'd let my ego, my pride or my stubborn streak block my vision and keep me trapped in an old way of thinking. You could, so easily, be reading a story about loss, when actually to me this is a tale of triumph and the amazing ability of ANY entrepreneurs to turn a difficult situation into a spring board.

One thing for sure is that there will be people who have been by my side day in and day out since launch and who have always had my back. They'll be along for the ride of 2.0. A more systemised, better version of our creation.

It's time to disrupt again. Hold on… Here we go!

How to find your
genius zone

1. REFRAME YOUR IDEA OF PRODUCTIVITY Do you really work best at a desk between 9 and 5 with only a one-hour lunch break? If this isn't your optimum way of working, give yourself permission to change it!

2. STEP AWAY – LITERALLY At times of crisis, it's tempting to hover around the office and your team. Relocate for a day or, in my case, four weeks and see what impact it has on your own, and your team's, energy.

3. SWAP REACTIVENESS FOR RESPONSIVENESS There's a big difference! Giving yourself space and freedom doesn't mean you're ignoring problems but facing them with objectivity rather than an emotional outburst.

4. AWAKEN YOUR CURIOSITY Watch an obscure movie, spend the afternoon in the library, attend a public speaking event or sign up to a masterclass. Remember how amazing it feels to learn something new.

5. INVITE PEOPLE ALONG WITH YOU My partner and I both discovered our genius zones during our Byron Bay trip (cue: LOTS of brainstorming sessions!), and it was so amazing to have his company. Want to reboot your creativity? Float the idea past a friend or staff member. Do they want to come on an inspiring journey with you?

6. DON'T RUSH TO LEAVE YOUR GENIUS ZONE! You can stay here as long as you want to – in fact, permanently. I'm no longer in Byron but I've brought my genius zone home with me. A certain place may have helped you to discover it, but your GZ is a mindset – and you can stay there forever.

She took an
ending
and turned it into
a fresh
start

Chapter Ten

Reframing
The end

CHAPTER TEN

Reframing the end

Some days the absolutely unimaginable happens. On September 18, 2017, my darling dad left his body. As I was introducing my incredible, beautiful friend Bradley Trevor Greive at one of our *Collective Hub* Masterclasses, my resilient and incredible Daddo had a heart attack. Less than 30 hours earlier, I'd taken a photo of us together at his apple farm in Orange where he was cutting me some cherry blossom – an image full of so much love, joy, energy and laughter.

In the midst of all the trials and tribulations you've been reading about over the past nine chapters, I lost the man who taught me how to live out loud, break every rule – unapologetically – and buck the status quo in the first place.

Here I was, already dealing with a business on its knees, and then boom! Right in the middle of starting the process for the business sale I was facing heartbreak upon heartbreak. Not to mention the logistics of a funeral, probate and inheriting my dad's business (and some of the most dysfunctional and money-grabbing people I've ever come across… the likes of which I've never experienced and hope to never again).

Yet, even at the time of dad's death, when I still had the urge every morning to pick up the phone and call him, I felt a huge wave of gratitude. I was thankful for every lesson he taught me, and how I inherited his 'anything is possible' attitude. People often ask me where I got my entrepreneurial and rebellious spirit, and juggle-a-million-things-at-once, get-shit-done attitude from, and it took me a long time to realise that the apple doesn't fall far from the tree.

I was beyond grateful to have shared one of the most fun, heartfelt, close weekends ever with him. The Sunday before he passed, we talked and talked, and created unforgettable moments and memories. Because of this, even as

I planned his (out-with-a-bang!) funeral, I felt calm, peaceful and philosophical about the inspiration you can find in an ending, whether it's saying goodbye to someone you love, a vision of your business or a part of your identity.

On death: it's a very strange, funny thing, really. There are many emotions and sometimes I just want to say 'fuck right off' to the world. I have my way of dealing with it – meditation, exercise, quiet times, reading, hugs with my partner. And I'm okay. I'm good, really. I have no regrets. Nothing unsaid. Nothing not closed. BUT then there's this barrage of noise from outside.

It seems that very few people feel comfortable about the notion of endings and so, socially, we don't make it okay – even for the person who is facing it. Of course, we all have the best intentions. Everyone, from those people who ring and just say, "I don't know what to say…" and then leave silence so I need to fill it. Excruciating! Then, there are the people who tell you over and over, "You must be DEVASTATED," as if that's useful. Or, when you say, "I'm okay," they reply, "Oh, it'll hit you soon…"

Some reactions, without even meaning to, have made us laugh until we cried. Dad's neighbour, when told, simply said, "Oh, my cat died this morning, too."

Less than three weeks after the funeral, I met my friend Jamie for a movie. As he arrived at my house to collect me, I was sitting there writing a potential topic for a new book. He laughed when he saw the title scrawled across my notebook: 'People are dodgy as f*ck around death'. Maybe not the most sensible title, but the sentiment was there.

It's been an interesting distraction, in a way, watching other people's behaviour around our family – their awkwardness, their shyness, their lack of words and their unnecessary, wholly un-beneficial dramatics. I've always been a natural observer and can't help analysing how our lives would be far easier if we realised endings are inevitable and learnt to embrace them. If we felt the pain – that does seem unbearable at times – but, instead of clinging to it, we allowed it to wash over us.

This is what I wrote in my journal around dad's passing:

"Arrrgggghhhhhh, deal with it people. Embrace. Learn. Go deep. Be unafraid. Be conscious. Do things differently. Just let yourself fucking be. Let it be okay. Don't cling on. Do away with the 'if onlys' and 'what ifs'. They are a fucking waste of time and they will drive you mad. Completely mad. Bonkers. Off the richter scale! They will not serve you and they will only take you down."

In the past 18 months I have said goodbye to my father and now I face another goodbye, as I prepare to announce the closure of the print magazine. I had no prior reference, compass, or way of knowing how I'd deal with these situations. But it's weird – I don't feel sad for either any more. I feel strong. I feel ready! I feel my dad around me, in every cell of my being.

During the editing process of this book, my sister and I have been cleaning our dad's apartment out. As a 'stuff-loather' the thought of going through all of his belongings nearly paralysed me. But my sister insisted that it would be cathartic. While she was much better at the detail than me, and I was mainly moral support, it was wonderful. Truly wonderful. As we shifted through Dad's stuff (realising he was SUCH a hoarder!), every item seemed to carry an unexpected message.

The guy had literally kept EVERY SINGLE ITEM he had ever been given; more than 2000 boxes of matches collected from every far-flung corner of the globe, every mobile phone bagged up separately, every shampoo from every hotel room he'd stayed in around the world and probably close to 500 pens. This taught me a few things. We can't take it with us. None of it. So don't hang onto things. Use them and then let them go.

Then there were things of importance... The other beautiful thing that came with Dad's hoarding was (god love him!) that he had meticulously kept every single issue of *Collective Hub*, every media clipping I was ever in and every single handwritten letter and postcard that I had ever given him. And, a mix-tape of me, him and my sister – but mostly ME – recording my own radio show when I was about seven. THIS was an incredible find. It all seemed so symbolic – let go of the stuff, and don't worry about the material. But find a way – any way – to preserve your memories and a legacy; the important things that make us who we are, the little signs that lead to our purpose.

The pièce de résistance was a copy of my first book *Daring & Disruptive*, which I'd gifted to him. Inside the front cover I'd scrawled, "Dad, thanks for always believing in me and inspiring me... Your daring and disruptive daughter." In that moment, I knew – without doubt – that nothing could hold me or my purpose down for long, and the best was yet to come!

Which brings me to where I am now... re-reading this book for the final time, as we send the final issue of *Collective Hub* to print (for now, anyway!), after telling my staff and our community about the new plans for its future. Amazingly, I feel amazing. To no surprise, my team have risen to the challenges of going out with a bang, by creating an issue that we're all incredibly proud of. And I've been overwhelmed by the support of our incredible community, all of our suppliers, distributors and the brands who love us and have supported us from the beginning. I'm so happy YOU all seem as excited as I am about the next chapter.

I know there may be times when my optimism may waver, just for a moment, and that's okay, too. I know I have the tools, rituals and attitude flips to be able to deal with it. The point is, endings don't scare me. If you allow them, they can liberate you. My dad's death has fuelled me and propelled me to live – to live a MUCH bigger, much more purposeful life full of freedom and choice and meaning and vitality. I feel like I have been here, in various iterations through my life – giving up drinking, launching *Collective Hub* and nearly losing it, relationship break-ups and now Dad – every one of those things has been shocking and nearly sunk me to my knees. But adversity can also give you strength and meaning. THIS is where the magic happens IF we're brave enough to let it pulse and vibrate through our very being.

There are other incredible lessons I've learnt from loss, both in the business and personal sense, over the past turbulent, jaw-dropping and constantly changing 18 months:

X   ALWAYS STAY HUMBLE Don't take anything for granted. In the past year, I've downsized every aspect of my life – my business, my home and a lot of my possessions, some out of choice and some out of necessity. There are many people who've had a lot more than me and lost a lot more than me, too. It's so important to always stay humble, grounded and unattached to material possessions (especially in the social media age where appearances can be deceptive). Without doubt, 100 per cent of my GREATEST times in the past few years have been the special intimate moments with my partner, family and friends that don't cost a cent. That's comforting to remember when anything you own is lost or failing.

X   LOYALTY GOES A LONG WAY I know this now more than ever. There's no way I would have survived the past year without the friends and confidants I've cried with, collapsed with and laughed with. You know who you are and (I hope!). I will stand by you forever. I've expressed my gratitude to every single one of you. Nearly losing so much has also taught me an incredible amount about compassion, empathy and the need to put yourself in someone else's shoes before judging them. We're all doing the best we can!

BE IN THE PRESENT As I have said many times before, thank goodness entrepreneurs seem to have this default setting of eternal optimist and an ability to quickly forget just how tough things are (or have been). I try, very consciously, to live in the present as much as possible. The alternative – dwelling on what's behind you – is not beneficial to anyone. There's nothing wrong with watching a 'highlight reel' of the day's events, but don't get stuck on a permanent re-run.

STAY JOYOUS Through all of this I've never stopped laughing. Even when I've been on my knees, it's incredible how one comment, one sight, sound or comical realisation can switch me, in an instant, from a snotty, sobbing heap into a moment of total hilarity. Like the red bucket getting stuck under my car, or my dog Benny pooping in the corner of the office in the middle of an investor meeting (talk about symbolism!). It's okay to laugh, even (especially!) in the midst of chaos.

DON'T FIGHT THE FLUX I've become surprisingly comfortable in a permanent state of flux. The flux of selling (and then not selling) the business, the flux of moving into and out of offices, the flux of moving in and out of houses and then, of course, Dad dying and my sister and I sorting through all of his STUFF and a rather confusing inheritance. Yet, somehow, I have managed to glide through a great deal of it relatively effortlessly. Perhaps this is the true nature of resilience – when so much just keeps coming at you day after day after day after day, you just become more able to deal with it – with practise.

Embracing impermanence

I guess the point is to always adopt an attitude of gratitude and maintain emotional tools and healing rituals to navigate through any life hurdles. Trust the process. Trust that an ending ALWAYS signals a new beginning or pivotal life lesson. There's really nothing to fear when you stop fighting change and instead allow yourself to be carried on to the next part of your journey.

As I type this it's almost six years since the idea behind *Collective Hub* was born. When I launched, it was the most disruptive play. It was fun. It was wild. I didn't think we would make it to issue three – but here we are. Issue 51 lands tomorrow and issue 52 is pretty much done and dusted. Now THAT feels like an incredible accomplishment. All dreamt up by someone who did 'veggie English' at school, had no magazine or media experience, no money, no smarts and a team of three all under the age of 25. Now you tell me that you can't do anything you put your mind to in this world.

After nearly 6000 or so interviews and articles with extraordinary brands, creatives, intrapreneurs and entrepreneurs from all over the planet, traversing industries and geographic locations, we've learnt more than I can put into words. Now it's time for us to go and explore – what's next? There's so much out there and so many amazing ways to change the world. It's time to lift, explore, and be open to creating magic at an entirely different level.

My dad lived larger than anyone I know. Like a snowball, he just kept gathering friends. He was loved and adored by thousands. Yet, even after he was gone, I still felt his presence strongly: guiding me in different ways, inspiring me, and pushing me forward. Even if I can't see him physically, I hope, and I believe, that the same will be true of *Collective Hub* its next iteration. I still don't think our investment opportunities are dead.

The co-founder of Airbnb still sends me private messages on Instagram. I'm still having conversations with amazing people who did dearly want to support us, but couldn't because of budgets, conflicting commitments or just because it was the wrong timing. There's still a great need in the world for a vehicle that drives optimism, hope, faith and inspiration. There's still a market of people desperately seeking a support system to lift them higher and ignite their full potential.

Though we're pressing print on our final issue (for now), that's not to say we won't bring out a few 'one-offs' each year with the best of the best – it's highly possible! I know for certain I will continue to bring *Collective Hub*'s 'anything is possible' message to our existing community and the new breed of game-changers, thought-leaders, style-makers, and risk-takers who are yet to emerge from their university lecture halls, corporate corner offices and inner-city cafés.

As for me, I've made personal pledges for the year ahead: to focus on my personal brand, to leverage the things I love and to continue to support you as best as I can. It's what makes 95 per cent of the money, however, it has been put on the backburner for the past two years.

I'll be surrounding myself with the best of the best, but everyone will work on a project by project basis, bringing together specialists not generalists. Many of my team from the past six years will be reuniting for parts of this journey – bringing the best of the band back together, as it were. Loyalty goes a LONG way and I will continue to support and give work to, and take on the journey well into the future those who have supported me.

I've also vowed to feed my curiosity, especially in the tech arena. So expect to see my face, front and centre, at all the upcoming tech conferences. It's time to become a student again – and I can't wait! Part of the plan is also to work smarter, not harder. And leaner but bolder, with lower costs but greater output and connection to community. Watch this space as, through whatever medium I choose to communicate, I plan to take you all on my journey – as always!

As I said at my dad's funeral, "Here's to the crazy ones, the misfits, the rebels, the troublemakers, the round pegs in the square holes... the ones who see things differently – they're not fond of rules... you can quote them, disagree with them, glorify or vilify them, but the only thing you can't do is ignore them because they change things... they push the human race forward, and while some may see them as the crazy ones, we see genius, because the ones who are crazy enough to think that they can change the world, are the ones who do."

I used this Steve Jobs quote in the first issue of *Collective Hub* and in my first book in this series, *Daring & Disruptive*. Today, it seems more relevant and important than ever, not just for me but for everyone chasing a dream and following their purpose or passion.

We all leave a legacy, whether it's to change one person's life or millions of people in a global community. You can never really lose anything that was once close to your heart. Your relationship just changes and you interact with it on a different level, through different channels. I've just got to get through this and keep putting one foot in front of the other. I am strong. I am resilient. I can do anything. And you can, too.

My dad and his stories will live on.

Just as *Collective Hub* and its stories will live on through our community.

Tomorrow is another day...

Break the rules.
Break your brand.
Break your own heart.

Sometimes
you have to shatter
stuff to rebuild it
stronger

Epilogue

EPILOGUE

*D*ear Start-up Community: entrepreneurs, intrapreneurs, creatives, game-changers, thought-leaders, rule-breakers, style-makers... our inspiration, our sole reason for being. In life, nothing stays the same – and who would want it to? We pivot, we evolve, we grow, we learn. This is truly the magic of entrepreneurship. Today, you and I have to stop and ask ourselves, 'Is this really my greatest calling going forward? Could there be a bigger, bolder, smarter way?' The truth? We've all got some brave decisions to make in the future, fellow disruptors. Sometimes, breaking a brand can remake it. And so we have big news...

This is the message we posted on the cover of issue 52 of *Collective Hub*, released into the world on March 26, 2018, the day we revealed the news the print magazine was closing. We could have gone out quietly, we could have purposefully chosen to wrap up the final issue as under-the-radar as possible. But, as a founder, I've built the entire *Collective Hub* community on the belief that we should live our lives out loud, boldly and bravely. It felt wrong to try to sweep the print magazine's closure under the rug. Plus, for our community this felt like a unique learning opportunity.

And so we decided to break every rule in the book (again!). Instead of featuring a high-profile person on our cover, my editor Amy and I decided we needed to do something very different – and very in tune with *Collective Hub*'s ethos. An open letter to our community, stripped back, unstyled and raw. This wasn't a goodbye; it was a pep talk, a tough-love speech and a warning!

In my Founder's Letter, which ran over six pages in this issue, I laid it out for our community: "The truth is that, as a rebellious and innovative founder, carving a new path in an industry verging on crumbling (I believe NO industry is immune to this), there are going to be periods when things don't go your way. At that point, you can either be led by your ego and cling onto the current iteration of your creation – and probably go under completely – or pivot, adapt and morph into a new way of being. One that stays true to your purpose, but is bigger, bolder and more sustainable."

I'll never forget going to bed the night before 'drop day', knowing the cover would be released at 7am the following morning across social media, the *Collective Hub* website and my new website LisaMessenger.com. Would we get slammed by the media? Would our community see it as a failure? Would our loyal and loving readers feel deserted? Was I scared? That's an understatement!

To accompany the cover drop, my editor Amy and I shot a video explaining the decision. Shot in one take, with minimal edits, I wanted our community – and the industry – to understand the print magazine's closure should not be viewed as a failure but proof that, to remain on purpose, you have to pivot, morph and ride out a storm in any way necessary.

I suspected the news of our closure – and how we were breaking it – would cause a big reaction. But even I underestimated its impact. I have a chart that shows the traffic to *Collective Hub*'s website that morning – and the mountainous spike that caused our page views to break all of our previous records. "I should close the magazine every day," I joked to my team, as we watched the comments under our social-media post multiply.

Part of me (a big part!) didn't want to read the comments, or the article that sprung up about our closure, but I knew facing people's reactions was part of my journey – and I owed it to everyone who took the time to write to us.

Over the next 48 hours, I attempted to read every email that landed in my inbox, every text message I received from a friend or acquaintance, every social media comment left and every blog post written by a commentator. The collective response from people I knew personally, and from strangers, brought me to tears – for all the right reasons.

I wish I could copy and paste every single response that I received here, but it would take up another 12 chapters to include them all. The outpouring of love was incredible; the influx of support was overwhelming and the love I felt was heart-expanding.

As the news spread, people wrote to me from across the world to say they were so sorry to hear about the print magazine but, more importantly, CONGRATULATIONS! It was a testament to our incredible community that, rather than seeing the print magazine's closure as a reason to be mournful, they saw it as a reason to celebrate the courage, determination, power and purpose it took to make such a hard decision.

As one email that I received read: "Sadness, complete admiration, pride, love, bravery, guts, innovation, authenticity, inspiring (so very much so), clever, trail-blazer, mentor, amazing, heartfelt, strong, human, real, relatable and one of a kind. These are just some of the words that come to my mind, as I think of you and your announcement."

Another email from a fellow founder read: "Too many people pretend like business is the easiest thing ever, all smooth sailing and expensive brunches and Instagram photos… I especially wanted to say thank you for everything you have done for me with *Collective Hub*. You have made such a difference not just to my business, but to my life and outlook."

Every word of support and gratitude filled a gap in my heart and re-nourished me. I'm not saying that week was easy. After making the decision to decentralise my team and find a new way of working remotely, we packed up and moved out of the office. This led to a three-hour sob-fest on my part, which I obviously needed as part of my healing process. ("It's okay," I told my partner when he caught me weeping unglamourously on the bathroom floor. "It's a good thing. I'm excited for the future.") I was actually so relieved that I could finally cry, let it out after 18 months of holding it in. I know there's practically nothing more powerful and it felt incredibly cathartic. It was exactly what I needed to do.

I felt so many deep emotions during that week. Yet, by the end of the process, after every supplier had been paid, every subscriber had been reimbursed and every contributor had been informed, I felt two overwhelming emotions – pride and gratitude! By making the tough call, putting my ego to one side, and sharing our ending honestly and transparently, we had bowed out gracefully and maintained the loyalty of our followers (who couldn't wait to hear what was next for us).

We offered our subscribers the chance to get a refund for the issues of the magazines they wouldn't receive, or the option to receive a copy of this book and access to an upcoming Masterclass instead – and 83 per cent of people chose the second option. I was blown away by their loyalty, empathy and commitment to remaining part of our future.

Most importantly, we had transformed our closure into a learning opportunity for our community. That week, I received countless emails from founders, creatives and game-changers in the start-up scene (many of whom ran successful companies – or so I thought), admitting they were also standing at a crossroads, career-wise, and that our video had helped them to make a tough decision.

One of my favourite responses read: "BRAVO! I just finished reading the magazine. There is ALWAYS a choice! Yes, yes, yes, absolutely always. And it is the warriors among us who feel it, see it and do it! Congrats on your pivot and shoving that human ego into the backseat where it belongs."

Another email I'll keep forever, read: "I love that you remind us to see change as positive. Your news today has already, I am sure, caused so many within your community to pause, reflect and learn a little more about themselves. I am so happy that you are free – zig when others are zagging – and I cannot wait to see what is in store once the dust settles."

It was also an incredible privilege to see my team roll with the changes, during a week that was just as big for them as it was for me. Proving that anything really is possible, and that you can choose how to react in the face of adversity, they closed the print magazine with as much passion as we launched it, determined to leave a positive legacy behind afterwards.

Despite losing a LOT of money by closing the magazine (people have no idea how much it costs to shut a business!) I never doubted my decision for a moment. In fact, I felt freer than I'd felt for years.

As I write this, only a month has passed since *Collective Hub*'s announcement. It's too early to reveal exactly what the future holds for us, as I want to give myself the time and space to explore all the amazing options that are unfolding (who knew closing a business could attract so many business opportunities?).

Needless to say, I have BIG plans, some of which may have come into fruition by the time you read this book. For now, I'm excited to have a chance to stop, get quiet, reflect, educate myself and have time and space to think outside the box again… or, in this case, to think outside of a conventional magazine format.

As I type this, I'm on a plane to Bali with my partner for some much-needed relaxation, restoration and creative inspiration, after the most emotional month and hardest year of my career.

I'm proud to be one of the many start-up survivors who has been pushed to their limits, and risen in the face of adversity. To anyone living this now, you WILL get through this. There is always an alternative. Anything really is possible, believe me. And, there's a lot to be said for plan B.

Sometimes we've just got to be courageous enough to break a few things and start over…

Here's to a leaner, smarter, brighter future.

Much love,

Lisa

ASK YOURSELF...
Am I still on
PURPOSE?
Follow your heart.
Trust your instinct.
DISRUPT

@LISAMESSENGER

About Lisa Messenger

Lisa Messenger is the vibrant, game-changing founder and CEO of *Collective Hub*. She launched *Collective Hub* as a print magazine in 2013 with no experience, in an industry that people said was either dead or dying. Over the next five years, *Collective Hub* grew into an international multimedia business and lifestyle platform with multiple verticals across print, digital, events and a co-working space – all of which served to ignite human potential.

Since the final print edition of *Collective Hub* in 2018, Lisa has continued to inspire game-changers, thought-leaders, style-makers, entrepreneurs and intrapreneurs across the world. An international speaker and best-selling author, she is an authority on disruption in both the corporate sector and the start-up scene.

Lisa's experience in publishing has seen her produce over 400 custom-published books for companies and individuals as well as having authored and co-authored 24 herself. Most notably, Lisa chartered her ride to success with her best-selling book *Daring & Disruptive: Unleashing the Entrepreneur* and its sequels, which includes *Life & Love: Creating the Dream,* which reached the number one spot on Booktopia; *Money & Mindfulness: Living in Abundance,* that shot to best-selling status within the first month; and *Break-ups & Breakthroughs: Turning an Ending Into a New Beginning* soon followed. As did *Purpose.*

Her passion is to challenge individuals and corporations to get out of their comfort zones, find their purpose, change the way they think, and to prove there is more than one way to do anything. She encourages creativity, innovation, an entrepreneurial spirit and lives life to the absolute max. Most mornings she wakes up and pinches herself at how incredible her life is, but is also acutely aware and honest about life's bumps and tumbles along the way.

With fans including Sir Richard Branson and New York Times best-selling author Bradley Trevor Greive, and a social media following of over 150,000, Lisa's vision is to build a community of like-minded people who want to change the world.

In between being a serial entrepreneur and avid traveller, she loves nothing more than being at home with her dog, Benny, gardening and collecting as many indoor plants as humanly possible.

@LISAMESSENGER

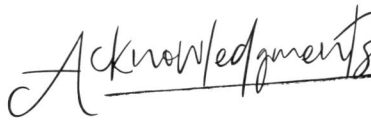

TO MY WONDERFUL, INSPIRING AND TENACIOUS TEAM:

Thank you to my team – every single one of you, past and present, who have created and worked tirelessly on this dream. You are like family and I will be forever grateful for your selflessness, loyalty and love for what we created with *Collective Hub*, and continue to create together in it's next iteration. There will be tough times and highs and lows, but having you all by my side every day makes the purpose and vision unwavering and unshakable. Knowing we have a combined purpose and a 'why' and are working together to achieve that is the greatest reason to get up every day.

TO THE PEOPLE IN MY LIFE WHO MAKE EVERYTHING BETTER:

To my family that forever keeps me grounded, to my incredible partner who's by my side every day, inspiring and guiding me. And, of course, to all my amazing, wonderful friends who make life full of colour. I love you.

TO THE ONES LIVING THEIR WHY OUT LOUD

To the thought leaders, change makers and rule breakers living their why out loud and proud – the ones who inspire me every day without even knowing it. To our *Collective Hub* community, this book is for you. Thank you for believing in us.

Speaking Opportunities

Lisa is available for speaking opportunities. Her key message is 'Anything is possible'. Her keynotes are highly engaging, energetic and really get audiences raring to face, and overcome, any new challenges head on. Using self-deprecating humour and colourful anecdotes you'll hardly believe, Lisa will take your audience on an incredible journey. Some of her speaking topics include:

Cultivating a killer self-belief

Finding passion and purpose

Creating an amazing team culture

Failing fast

Strategic partnerships

Thinking big and going global

Challenging your personal limits and overall thinking

Building a personal brand or business

Disrupting in business and within a corporate

Developing a sixth sense

Investing in yourself

FOR MORE INFORMATION, BOOKINGS AND BULK BOOK SALES
ENQUIRIES, EMAIL LISA@LISAMESSENGER.COM

Other books by Lisa

AVAILABLE AT SELECTED NEWSAGENTS, BOOKSTORES, TRAVEL + AIRPORT STORES OR VISIT COLLECTIVEHUB.COM

Collective Hub launched in 2013 as a print magazine in 37 countries, and quickly became a global sensation. It evolved into a true international multimedia business and lifestyle platform that encompassed engaging digital content, bespoke events, strategic collaborations and unique product extensions. Across it all, *Collective Hub*'s vision and purpose was to ignite human potential, and this mission will continue in any form the brand takes. Everything we produce exists to inspire and educate people on how to become the best versions of themselves so that no human potential goes wasted. Combining style and substance with a fresh perspective on the issues that matter most, *Collective Hub* covered business, design, technology, social change, fashion, travel, food, film and art.

This ethos continues on LisaMessenger.com, an online portal for inspiring books, articles, digital masterclasses, virtual events, collaborations and more.

More than anything, *Collective Hub* was created to bring game-changers, thought-leaders, style-makers, entrepreneurs and intrapreneurs together. We offer pragmatism and inspiration in equal measure to help create a world of dreamers and doers. Join our community and unlock the best version of yourself.

COLLECTIVEHUB.COM
@LISAMESSENGER #LISAMESSENGER
@COLLECTIVEHUB #COLLECTIVEHUB

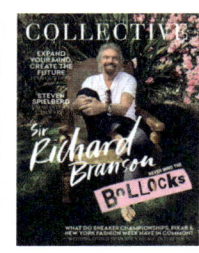

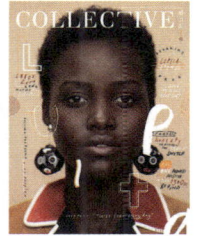
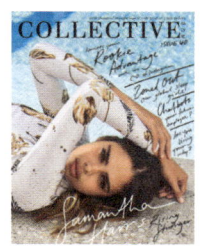

She took
an
ending
and turned
it into a
fresh start

@LISAMESSENGER